BRAVE MOMS,

brave kids

LEE NIENHUIS

HARVEST HOUSE PUBLISHERS
EUGENE, OREGON

BRAVE MOMS, BRAVE KIDS

Copyright © 2017 Lee Nienhuis
Published by Harvest House Publishers
Eugene, Oregon 97408
www.harvesthousepublishers.com

ISBN 978-0-7369-7003-7 (pbk.)
ISBN 978-0-7369-7004-4 (eBook)

Library of Congress Cataloging-in-Publication Data

Names: Nienhuis, Lee, author.
Title: Brave moms, brave kids : a battle plan for raising heroes / Lee
   Nienhuis.
Description: Eugene, Oregon : Harvest House Publishers, 2018. | Includes
   bibliographical references.
Identifiers: LCCN 2017029351 (print) | LCCN 2017048676 (ebook) | ISBN
   9780736970044 (ebook) | ISBN 9780736970037 (pbk.)
Subjects: LCSH: Christian education of children. | Christian education—Home
   training. | Mother and child—Religious aspects—Christianity. | Child
   rearing—Religious aspects—Christianity. | Parenting—Religious
   aspects—Christianity. | Mothers—Religious life.
Classification: LCC BV1475.3 (ebook) | LCC BV1475.3 .N54 2018 (print) | DDC
   248.8/45—dc23
LC record available at https://lccn.loc.gov/2017029351

Printed in the United States of America

17 18 19 20 21 22 23 24 25 / VP-GL / 10 9 8 7 6 5 4 3 2 1

Contents

To Brendan, Gabriella, Lexie Beth, and Ryan

The wonder of it all is that I get to be your mama. There are no words to describe this honor. With all my heart I pray:

"That according to the riches of his glory he may grant you to be strengthened with power through his Spirit in your inner being, so that Christ may dwell in your hearts through faith—that you, being rooted and grounded in love, may have strength to comprehend with all the saints what is the breadth and length and height and depth, and to know the love of Christ that surpasses knowledge, that you may be filled with all the fullness of God."
—*Ephesians 3:16-19*

I love you.

A Word from the Author

What you hold in your hands is a gamble, truly—an act of faith on my part. I am in the throes of motherhood, so deeply buried in the trenches of the everyday that I don't dare take my eyes off my own mission. Four little people rely on me for everything from rides to practice and new shoes to bath time and a competitive Candy Land opponent. I am not done with my journey. I am not looking back with fondness over each step. I am right in the middle of my walk of faith in *this generation*, through the grit of the day with the trials of this fast-paced society and dark world.

There is still ample time for my kids to fall apart. Although they are making age-appropriate decisions to follow Christ today, tomorrow they could hit some rough patch and skid out of control. We never, ever know what a day will bring, do we? But as one of the wisest women I know once told me, "If you think you have motherhood figured out, one of two things could happen. You could become *paranoid* when it isn't going as planned. Or you could become *proud*. Both of those bring displeasure to God, Lee." Not having ultimate control could drive me crazy or it could drive me to my knees in prayer. I am choosing the latter.

Let's just address the risk right from the start. First, I could still mess up my kids. I am totally aware that I have an everyday fight against my own sin, and that surely in our close proximity the kids will take shrapnel from my own battle. If you were looking for a book

9

written by a perfect parent, it's best for you to disengage now. I assure
you, rarely do a couple of days go by that I don't wish I could redo
a conversation or an interaction. You can't talk as much as I do and
not dig yourself into a hole occasionally.

Yet I've produced children just like me, sinners desperately in need
of the grace of Jesus. So the broken mother is part of this equation, but
the broken kid is part of it as well.

Although all signs are good right now, my kids could still choose
to walk away from the God their dad and I love so much. They might
not choose dynamic faith, or faith at all. Experience tells us when children leave home, all bets are off. They make the choices about what
they will believe and who they will become. We've all seen it happen—
godly families with prodigals. The idea could slay me.

These are the concerns I have wrestled with extensively. When it
came to finally writing this book, I felt all the *what ifs* and fear whispered, "*Unqualified.*" But down at the core of me, I believe that anything God has called me to do He will equip me to do. I am a student
of God's Word, and in the Bible He laid out principles that must be
followed for us to raise up another generation of Christ followers. His
Word contains everything I need for life, godliness, and courageous
motherhood and everything my kids need for life, godliness, and
dynamic faith (2 Peter 1:3-4). My hope is not in my own strength,
but in His. And I am going to do this afraid because I'm still feeling
the butterflies along with the thought, *Surely there is someone else.* A
quick trip through Scripture and history assures me most heroes are
afraid at the beginning and maybe all the way to the end. They just
choose to do it anyway.

> This is my prayer: that your love may abound more and
> more in knowledge and depth of insight, so that you may
> be able to discern what is best and may be pure and blame-
> less for the day of Christ, filled with the fruit of righteous-
> ness that comes through Jesus Christ—to the glory and
> praise of God (Philippians 1:9-11 NIV).

Part One

Tired of Being Afraid

*In every great story is a defining moment, a time when
a decision changes everything. This is our moment.*

1

Where Are All the Heroes?

Since it is so likely [children] will meet cruel enemies,
let them at least have heard of brave
knights and heroic courage.
—C.S. LEWIS

The scene is dark and creepy. If there were background music it would be filled with dissonance, that eerie sound exactly the opposite of harmony. Unresolved tension leads us to feel in our very marrow how far we've traveled from where we are supposed to be. Danger lurks around every corner with enemies lying in wait to spring out in surprise. And just when it feels as though the danger has been avoided, a new, even scarier enemy or trap pops up.

What lurks around the next corner? Whom should I fear?

I change the channel on movies like this. I've never been the girl who wanted to be afraid on purpose. I'd take a good underdog story *any* day of the week over a creepy movie that leaves me feeling restless and unresolved. That's what dissonance is, after all. The problem is this isn't a movie. This is today.

Everyone is wondering when the hero will show up to do something about all this darkness and evil, but there's no symbol we can shoot into the sky to bring someone to the rescue. If only it were that simple.

Dissonance: "lack of harmony among musical notes";
"a tension or clash resulting from the combination of
two disharmonious or unsuitable elements"[1]

The dark scene greets us every morning. It's my town and it's yours. The world spins and warps as one natural disaster after another hits and weather forecasters remind us we are breaking every historical record. It's almost as though we are operating only in the areas of extremes. Not just in the weather, but in the volatility of the stock market, the place many of us trust with our financial investments, plans, and provision for the future. We've watched an entire hard-working generation lose their footing and sense of security in a couple of lousy days on Wall Street. Rising costs at the grocery store make us shake our heads and wonder how we will continue to feed our children well. And then there is the matter of evil—pornography, drug abuse, embezzlement, misuse of power and office.

We are in a time of redefinition of marriage and when the moral compass seems to have lost its needle altogether. Personal integrity, modesty, and purity seem archaic, as though those are words from a different century. While we may believe conceptually that such traits are best for our children, such attributes considered old-fashioned will undoubtedly open them up to shaming and mockery.

Perhaps it has always been this way, and now our eyes have been opened to the darkness. Or maybe the dark's rage is getting stronger. Jesus warned us that "in the world [we] will have tribulation" (John 16:33), but the reality of these trials seems so strong now. Is it just me or do Christians say now more than ever, "It's only going to get worse, you know"?

I woke up this morning to news of another mass shooting. It troubles me that I'm no longer shocked by the daily reports; they all seem common now. I pour myself another cup of coffee and prepare for another day of raising children in a violent world. Some days I want to scream, "Stop the madness!" and quit watching the news, or grab every one of our elected officials and say, "Do something!" I want to shout at the church and issue a rally cry to everyone I know. "Pray! We must pray!" On the ugliest days, when everything inside me quakes, I want to dig a hole in the backyard to hide in, gather my babies, rock them, and cry, "Come, Lord Jesus. Please, come."

This is not the world we wanted for our children. For pity's sake, in 2012 a man walked into Sandy Hook Elementary School in Connecticut and shot first graders. The next day I had friends researching bulletproof vests for their children and backpacks that doubled as body armor. We watched the news of parents frantic to find their children, and our hearts became like lumps in our throats. For days, I held my kids, prayed for the parents whose children would never come home, and wondered to myself, *What kind of evil shoots children?*

When I was growing up, wars happened on the other side of the world. Iraq was a land far, far away, and my dad, who was a retired lieutenant colonel in the army, made me feel safe. He assured me that our country's military far surpassed them all and that we were protected. That's what dads do. But one Tuesday morning the rules of security changed forever. September 11, 2001, changed America's vocabulary. Men living inside our country, who were neighbors, had jobs, and went to the grocery store like the rest of us, orchestrated an attack that killed thousands of people before the bleary eyes of a nation. Some of us hadn't even had our morning cup of coffee. I sat with my husband and close friends and watched replay after replay of the Twin Towers collapsing, wondering who could possibly have done this and why. Why kill innocent people?

We all changed that day, whether we were in our twenties and heading to work (like me), or trying to feed breakfast to a house full of kids, or quieting a child. That was the day the word *terrorism* found its way into the vocabulary of our everyday and the façade of safety shattered around us.

Today my children practice "active shooter drills" in school. They pile up like puppies, hidden in closets and corners away from doors and windows, just in case. When my daughter came home and told me about it, my heart ripped wide open. We don't watch the news around here much, and I try not to focus our attention on the darkness, but it creeps into corners.

Then we have the matter of persecution. Twenty years ago, if we read these words, we may have nodded our heads, agreeing that hypothetically we could sometimes be insulted as Christians: "Blessed are you when people insult you, persecute you and falsely say all kinds of evil against you because of me. Rejoice and be glad, because great is your reward in heaven, for in the same way they persecuted the prophets who were before you" (Matthew 5:11-12 NIV).

You could get whiplash over how quickly times have changed, and today nothing is hypothetical about being insulted and misunderstood because you follow Christ. Self-identifying as a Christian is a surefire way to become a target for mockery, suspicion, and accusation. Snide remarks and disgusted glances, however, feel welcome when we look at businessmen and businesswomen who are now forced to choose between obeying the law of the land and violating their God-given consciences. Allowing faith to become a private matter to protect our families' futures is a real temptation.

And then we have "YouTube" martyrdom. We have no words for watching men dressed in orange jumpsuits, kneeling on a sandy beach, hooded men with long blades standing behind them. Our breath gathers into knots in our throats and tears sting our eyes because we know what comes next—heads are severed for the sake of the kingdom of God. This is the ultimate sacrifice in following the Lord Jesus. Men dressed in black, faceless, asking men if they will deny Christ. It feels unholy to look away and too much to process all at the same time.

This morning my five-year-old son stood at the other end of our church pew and sang the words to "I Have Decided to Follow Jesus" from the soles of his feet. His exuberance and conviction made the surrounding crowd turn and grin, and I'm certain also warmed them to the soles of their feet. I was proud of Ryan. My son *has* made the decision to follow Jesus, and as much as that sweet and spicy boy knows how, he *is* following Jesus. It's no small thing when your child declares his love for the Lord, publicly no less. But that pride and the tears of happiness that stung the corners of my eyes were soon replaced. The next line of that song says, "No turning back, no turning back." It could cost Ryan everything to follow Jesus, and that knowledge churns my stomach. I go back and forth between wanting to fist bump his dad in pride and excitement and wishing the following verse did not say, "The cross before me, the world behind me."

It will take a heroic effort to follow Christ in this generation and the next. Not too long ago I saw a sign in a rest area that said, "Looking for everyday heroes." I can't seem to let go of that phrase. Heroes don't wear capes and swoop in to save the day, and *hero* isn't a job description, no matter what the movies tell us. Heroism happens in a moment that you've trained for all your life. It's a revealing of the character stored up in you that meets the moment ordained for it to be revealed to the world. Years and years of practicing faithfulness has been stored up for the time it takes a stand.

 A hero is an ordinary individual who finds the strength to persevere and endure in spite of overwhelming obstacles. —Christopher Reeve[2]

What's a Hero, Anyway?

A hero is a faith-filled child of God who so believes in the goodness, worthiness, and faithfulness of God that she is obedient to His call on her life in public and private. Heroes are marked by integrity and a willingness to do the right thing when no one is watching. They are courageous—not foolish, but courageous—when fear could swallow them whole. They help when it hurts and stand when their knees shake. Heroes have strength and fortitude that hold firm when storms blow around them, knowing God's way is best despite opposition. They are willing to be used by God and allow Him to direct them into all that will entail. Heroes roll up their sleeves and get to work no matter how daunting the task in front of them. They are faithful and can be counted on to do the right thing, to cling tight to the Lord over and over. This is heroism, and if it has ever been needed, surely it is needed now.

The world pushes forward athletes and musicians who have been given big platforms and fame. But spotlights can be a distraction, and those who seek them can be easily knocked off-kilter. True heroes are people who do the right thing, whether or not anyone is watching.

Is it wishful thinking to hope Christian parents today can raise children who follow hard after their God? Do these kinds of people even exist anymore? It is so easy to be disenchanted and skeptical of all leaders. Our skepticism may have merit, but heroes of the faith are everywhere. We just need to know what we're looking for—and greater still, our children need to be trained to look for heroes and emulate them. Heroes won't always be the presidents of organizations, the ones giving speeches, or people with any accolades at all. They will be the faithful. The parents who hold coats over their kids' heads while it rains at the bus stop or the mom or dad kneeling in prayer when no one is watching. She may sit knee to knee with someone broken over loss, whispering the truth of Christ's power over that hurting heart. Or our hero may be a young man who says no to a temptation that nags again and again and again.

Heroes finish the race. They know it will be messy, bloody, and hard, but they refuse to give up on their God just because the journey is difficult.

Two Kinds of Mothers

I met a hero in the making at a family Christmas party this year. It isn't unusual for new people to be at our gatherings because the cousins are of marrying age and the grandkids sometimes bring friends. Sam, however, had no intention of marrying one of us—he is a foreign exchange student staying with my aunt and uncle. He introduced himself and told me he was from Mexico. He had planned on an exchange opportunity in Canada, but he was rerouted to Michigan. Canada's loss.

I could tell my aunt Jean was totally taken with this 17-year-old boy. Sam played games with the younger kids and made appropriate small talk with the adults. I remember thinking to myself what a cool guy he was. I had no idea what lay behind that engaging smile.

Jean and I found a spot to talk, and I asked her to tell me how the experience with Sam was going. She gushed about what a cool kid he was and explained how sad she was going to be when he left. He had rededicated his life to Christ at a youth event a few weeks before and had been loving his youth group. Sam had come out of a religious background and known the Lord, but he had not made the connection between heritage and personal, daily faith. I think that's why God sent him to Michigan.

Jean seemed eager to tell me his story. "Sam loves his country, Lee. He told me people think the Mexican people are lazy, but that they aren't." She assured him she knew that full well. She grew up on a fruit farm with migrant workers from Mexico coming to help bring in the crop. Jean worked side by side with many hardworking Mexicans. This must have bolstered his pride, because he explained, "Our television has shows that glorify the life of the drug lords. They have nice homes, fancy cars, and women. It's so wrong. What our people need instead of this way of life is confidence."

Sam is still developing where that confidence will find its grounding, but he wants to be a man who leads out of integrity and self-sacrifice. Jean leaned in. "Sam wants to be the president of Mexico." When he told each of his mamas—his own in Mexico and Jean in America—as much, the difference between their responses was like night and day. One spoke death to his dream and the other gave life to it. His mama in Mexico told Sam not to talk like that. "No, Sam. They kill the good men. You can't do that." Jean smiled over him and his plans and courageously whispered, "I believe you can."

> If I want to raise a hero, I'm going to have to *become* a hero, because brave kids need brave moms.

This is what we live for as mothers—the moment when our child turns to us and says, "I want to do something great with my life in the service of others." Or "I want to follow Christ wherever He leads." This is the heart cry of a hero, and what we learn at the very bottom of it all is this: If I want to raise a hero, I'm going to have to *become* a hero, because brave kids need brave moms. Heaven help me if my fear keeps my child from serving the Lord and becoming a change agent in our dark culture.

The sacrifice is real. The danger is real. Let's do it anyway.

Lord,

This world is frightening and changing quickly. At every turn the Enemy seems to be winning ground, and at times the task You've given me to raise wholehearted Christ followers seems out of reach. I'm so grateful we don't face the road ahead alone. Start in me, Lord. Mold me into the brave, faithful woman of God You have created me to be. Then use me to develop children who make an impact for the kingdom of God for Your name and glory. In Jesus's powerful name I pray, amen.

2

The Mama Prayer and When FEAR Sets In

*Being a mother is learning about strengths you didn't know
you had, and dealing with fears you didn't know existed.*
—LINDA WOOTEN[1]

We should have notified our family to invest in e.p.t. stock. The pregnancy test business picked up speed when Mike and I decided to start our family. Like so many other couples, we began to live on the 28-day roller coaster of "trying." Every four weeks my hopes for a baby grew, but the negative tests piled up. By the end of year two, we were past the point of having fun and relaxing and enjoying. Doubts abounded and my heart was raw. I was tired of hoping and tired of being emotionally spent.

> Hope deferred makes the heart sick, but a desire fulfilled
> is a tree of life (Proverbs 13:12).

One night during this season, I was lying in bed reading my Bible when a prayer from the book of Acts leapt off the page. "I commit you to God and to the word of his grace, which can build you up and give you an inheritance among all those who are sanctified" (Acts 20:32 NIV).

I was struck by the thought that if God ever did give us children, I would pray that prayer of consecration over them. As I look back I see that was the beginning of a shift inside me, a revelation that parenting ultimately was not designed to bring me joy and to have a little person who looked like me. I began to see parenting as a sacred trust from the Lord that was about raising another human being to love and glorify God. I marked the passage in my Bible and went back to it several times, committing our "hypothetical" children to the Lord.

Shortly thereafter, God allowed us to conceive. When the nurse called to let me know I was pregnant, she squealed as loudly as I did. The morning sickness began concurrently with that phone call. But from night one I prayed that the Lord would allow that tiny being to become a believer in Jesus as soon as he or she was able. We used a pregnancy journal to pray day by day for the physical development of that nausea-inducing member of our family. We prayed for eyes that would be able to see and appreciate the beauty the Lord made and know Him through it. A heart that would pump strong and have a spot just for Jesus. Hands, feet, organs.

It sounds so spiritual now as I write these words, but we had no idea what we were doing; we were just so astounded that God had allowed conception to happen. Mike read to my belly, and day in, day out we created a rhythm of seeking the Lord for our child until it was something we simply did, every day pleading with the Lord to allow our child to become a believer.

The day they laid our son in our arms, I realized it was possible for your very heart to live outside your body. Well, technically that didn't happen until after the hormone drop a few days later. Those first few days I was a mess of tears, trying to decide what would happen if the dog and the baby didn't mesh. Would I regret having a baby? Could I get rid of the baby? It is best to be attended to at all moments when you are that sleep deprived and hormonal. I wish I were joking about the last few sentences. Have mercy. He was so tiny and precious and made me need Jesus like I needed oxygen.

Maybe more so. Those first few months were a blur of firsts, but three people were born the day our son came into the world: Brendan, a proud father, and a mother.

We were just normal first-time parents. I took thousands of pictures, wrote down every first, and savored naptime. As Brendan grew, I tried to be faithful—not perfect, but faithful—to speak words of faith into his life. The next few years brought a difficult miscarriage and the adoption of our daughter, Gabriella. A couple of years after that brought another fertility treatment miracle, our Lexie Beth. Just when I thought I understood the limitations of my body and perhaps in some way thought I had the plan all figured out, I learned I was pregnant with our fourth child. No hormones, no drugs, no piles of tests—simply jaw-dropping surprise. Apparently, it really is that simple for some people, I surmised. Our son, Ryan, was born in an intense whirlwind of emotion and feelings—and by that I mean back labor and too late for an epidural.

Day in and day out we would do normal family stuff—potty training, trips to the park, and bedtime Bible stories. Each night would find us praying, again and again, that our children would come to know Jesus as their Savior. Then one day as we were driving down a back road, our oldest, who was four, began talking about heaven. That afternoon, at the edge of a cherry orchard, I was privileged to lead my son to Christ. Was he able to make decisions at that time about major theology and tenants of faith? No, but Brendan knew he was a sinner created by a God who wanted relationship with him. He knew Jesus came for him, died for him, and rose for him, and that he wanted to follow Jesus. That's the good stuff.

As my husband and I laid down that night for bed, I wondered aloud what we would pray now that the Lord had answered our prayers for our oldest. He was saved. Now what should I pray? It was a precious and holy moment as I pondered what came next. That's when the prayer began to form in my heart and mind. I didn't want my children to trust Christ only for salvation; I wanted them to be mighty warriors in the kingdom of God. My prayers morphed from "Get 'em saved" to a battle cry: "Get them ready, Lord!"

Warrior Prayers

My children, one by one, gave their little hearts to Jesus. Gabi and Lexie surrendered their hearts in their room during family devotions, and Ryan prayed with me when he was three at the kitchen table. All the while, every day found Mike and me praying strategically for each child. Until they accepted Christ as their Savior, we prayed they would yield their hearts to Him, and once they had, we prayed that God would use them and equip them to be mighty warriors in His kingdom.

I began praying that their hearts would always be turned toward Christ. I was asking for a passion to be ignited in them for the Word of God and His ways. We wanted them to be courageous soul winners who were prepared and eager to share the gospel, warriors who would stand alone for the cause of Christ and live for the glory of the Lord.

As I prayed, my faith increased, and I found myself believing that Jesus *would* use them. They would be useful to Him.

Safe

I can't put my finger on the exact moment when fear crept into my heart, but one day I took a brief survey of the world we're living in and an icy grip grabbed hold. I was praying that my kids would be warriors for Christ, but I realized just the term *warrior* indicated they would see war. People are hurt in war. Enemies are in war. Battles without promises of safety are in war. And as much as I believed Jesus was worth it, my mama heart began to latch onto the idea that I could somehow protect them better than He could. "Father, I know You love them, and I want You to use them to advance Your kingdom, but I want them safe."

I never intended to stop praying hero prayers for them; it's just that fear began to creep into the corners of my heart. I found myself afraid to continue praying for them to be boldly used by God. It felt as though I was painting a target on their backs for the Enemy to aim at. At night I began thinking of ways to skirt the brave prayers, so I'd stick to the basics: keep them safe, make them healthy, make them good friends, help them to love You. Not bad—completely necessary—but in my heart I knew I had moved to defensive prayer. Slowly, ever so slowly, my brave was melting away. I knew my concern for their safety was beginning to override my desire for them to live boldly for Christ.

Nearby

It wasn't only safety I was becoming concerned about. I frequently prayed that God would give my children a desire and heart for the world. We want to raise them up to go anywhere the Lord leads and do anything He asks of them. Mike and I have a deep love for missions and count it a privilege to call some close friends and family missionaries. As the kids have grown, we've often read missionary stories, watched movies, and interacted with our friends to help instill in them a love for people around the world. Somehow the idea seemed romantic in concept only until we watched people we love leave their families to follow Jesus across the globe. England. Brazil. Costa Rica. Indonesia and Thailand. China and Iraq. Those are only a few of the places where we have friends scattered around God's green earth.

As we've watched them go, part of me has cheered inside. "Yes, another generation that will love the Lord more than the security of home and the American dream!" We should cheer as heroes follow God's call. Then, in the next breath, my heart has churned. We want our kids to be close so we can enjoy them, admire them, and have a house full of people during the holidays. The bold prayer "Use them, Lord, to reach the world" began to morph into "as long as it is within driving distance of home."

Textbook

I want to know that if I do A, B, and C, then my children will turn out right. I want some assurance that loving God and loving them will be enough. I'm sure you want that too. We read passages like the one that says to "train up a child in the way he should go; even when he is old he will not depart from it" (Proverbs 22:6) and white-knuckle it until our hands bleed from clinging. I think that's what the Lord wants us to do, but maybe you're with me in desiring a more fool-proof formula.

Love God + Train them up = Smooth sailing with great kids

Experience and time have taught me that rarely do children make all their life choices according to a safe, predictable schedule. Bumps in the journey are inevitable even if we strive to do our best to raise them to know and honor the Lord.

"Why is my child so willful?"

"Why isn't he expressive or excited about his faith?"

"How could she act like that when we raised her so differently?"

All these and a thousand other questions rattle our minds as we raise our children. We want some guarantee that when all is said and done they will love Jesus and us. Hope turns so quickly into brokenness when their faith doesn't look the way we think it should. "Jesus, I know I said I want them to follow the path You have for them, but I'd prefer it went primarily straight, with very few curves, bumps, and dips."

Outlive Us

Four years ago, one of our closest friends was diagnosed with stage 4 liver cancer. The diagnosis was a death sentence—zero survivors after five years. Our friend, Ryan, made it two. Ryan was the marketing director of a Christian camp, married to his high school sweetheart, and they had a precious one-year-old son, Colton. Ryan was a mighty warrior in the kingdom of God, wise beyond his years. We had the honor of front-row seats from the night of his diagnosis until we said good-bye the day before he died. Watching his parents marked us forever. They were filled with faith and love for the Father, but still they grieved the painful road the Lord had chosen for them.

Ryan and his wife, Kendra, touched thousands of peoples' lives for Christ. They expressed unwavering hope, they boldly proclaimed the gospel, and they were faithful to point people to Jesus. We knew and recognized the undergirding of the Holy Spirit as we all walked that painful road together, and a deep truth settled over my heart. That the Lord may take my child from me if it will bring Him glory is a terrifying thought. He may not let them outlive me in a myriad of ways. Cancer, as for Ryan, an accident...we have no guarantee for tomorrow.

I felt the sting of this uncertainty the morning my youngest son was born. He stopped breathing and turned blue in my arms. I screamed for help and someone yelled, "Code blue!" over the PA system. What seemed like 30 nurses descended on our room. One nurse grabbed him from my arms and yelled, "Just give me the baby!" and then ran to the nursery. Most of the staff followed her, but three nurses stayed with me to make sure I was safe and calm. What followed was the longest 15 minutes of my life while I waited to hear news about my little one.

This time the news was wonderful. His lungs were suctioned and he went on to do just fine, but that event reminded me that I cannot breathe for my children. I can't add one breath to any of their lungs or one minute to their day. Only the Lord can do that. I would spend three months living on blessed little sleep, watching our little Ryan's chest rise and fall, willing it to continue. "Lord, I know I said 'anything to bring You glory,' but please don't take my child." Months later, the Lord reminded me He is the only one who knows the number of my children's days.

> My frame was not hidden from you when I was made in the secret place, when I was woven together in the depths of the earth. Your eyes saw my unformed body; all the

days ordained for me were written in your book before
one of them came to be (Psalm 139:15-16 NIV).

The problem we face as mothers is we cannot hold on to both fear
and faith simultaneously. I began to find the fear debilitating and suffocating. I realized the slide from anxiety into depression is well worn
by mothers who cannot function because they are chained to events
that haven't even happened. Some withdraw from society and cluster
into huddles of other believers, who curse the darkness and live reactionary, threatened lives. I began to see signs of that developing in me.

Where was the boldness that moved out in faith? My wild fear
began to lead to anger and rage because I hate being afraid. I didn't
know where to direct my frustration. God could prevent the events I
feared from happening, and why wouldn't He want to do that for us?
Has the whole world lost their ever-loving minds? I thought. The media,
who seemed to be whipping us all into a frenzy? My pastor, who was
preaching through the book of Revelation to make sure we'd know
the signs of the end times? Even my dreams began to be affected as
fear ran unchecked.

I was a ticking time bomb. A hurting, confused, desperately-want-
ing-to-please-the-Lord ball of emotions. Can you relate?

Lord,
My fear cannot run the show in my family. I thank You that al-
though the world screams loudly, You are on the throne and re-
main in control. Reveal to me areas where fear has gripped my
heart and help me to learn truth that combats it. You have created
this love and desire for the well-being of my children, but it cannot
become an idol I serve. Search my heart and show me places I have
surrendered to fear. In Jesus's name I pray, amen.

3

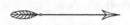

Fear Left Unchecked

*I have learned to kiss the wave that
slams me into the Rock of Ages.*
—Attributed to Charles Spurgeon

I love to listen to my girls' laughter. The sweet sound delights my heart to no end, and I often find myself becoming silly just to hear peals of it ring out. Recently, they received an unusual doll from the Caribbean islands that is dressed in a beautiful, tropical dress filled with bright colors and with a flowing skirt. If you pull the skirt up over the head of the Caribbean doll, you find underneath another woman dressed in a rich, dark-blue and purple gown. Two dolls in one. The hilarity begins when I hold the tropical doll right side up and say, "I am the most beautiful woman in the islands!" Of course, the doll underneath immediately raises the skirt and argues back, "No! I am the most beautiful. Look at my dress. I am beautiful, beautiful." She, of course, has righted herself and hidden the other doll beneath her skirt. The argument and two-sided doll pageant has been performed countless times since her arrival in our home.

The doll is a reminder that sometimes an issue does have two sides. Fear is also a two-sided species. One side is beneficial, life-giving, and even useful; the other side is dark, consuming, and leads to death.

The entrance of fear into my life was surprising. I'd always

29

29

considered myself a risk taker, bold in faith, willing to push limits and always up for an adventure. But when our fears threaten our children, we have an altogether different reaction. Anxiety can creep deep into a mother's heart and threaten to undo her. That is exactly what fear and anxiety are designed to do—overtake us.

Yes, I said *designed*. I have become absolutely convinced that fear is a created entity designed not by Satan as we might suppose, but rather by a perfect, all-knowing, always-loving God. When God created Adam and Eve, they were given the emotion of fear. This powerful emotion was meant to fill them with awe and wonder, to stop them cold and leave them slack-jawed. Fear was a beautiful, powerful feeling designed to make them worship the object of their fear. This is fear in the old biblical sense. *Holman Treasury of Key Bible Words* says, "The right fear of God leads to obedience and righteous living. Not to engender fear for fear itself."[1]

The scope of Adam and Eve's fear was from created to Creator. They were given the capacity to recognize God's right to rule over them, to set their boundaries, and to define their purpose. Unlike your standard-issue computer, which has no fear within it, we were created to recognize the implications of Someone so much greater than us in our presence. Fear makes us feel out of control, and it should. For anyone with any sense in the presence of God, the result should be deep humility and reverence. Before their fall, Adam and Eve interacted with God in submission and obedience out of reverence and love. Fear was not harmful; it was a gift.

As you well know, that's not the end of the story. When Adam and Eve made the decision to disobey God and usurp His right to rule over them, fear stepped in and did its job.

> When the woman saw that the fruit of the tree was good for food and pleasing to the eye, and also desirable for gaining wisdom, she took some and ate it. She also gave some to her husband, who was with her, and he ate it. Then the eyes of both of them were opened, and they realized they were naked; so they sewed fig leaves together and made coverings for themselves.

Then the man and his wife heard the sound of the
LORD God as he was walking in the garden in the cool
of the day, and they hid from the LORD God among the
trees of the garden. But the LORD God called to the man,
"Where are you?"

He answered, "I heard you in the garden, and I was
afraid because I was naked; so I hid (Genesis 3:6-10 NIV,
emphasis added).

Fear overcame Adam and Eve because they had taken themselves
out of the God-ordained order of authority. They were given the good
sense to know they had done wrong. Hear this: God intended for terror and dread to be associated with fear, but fear was created in love
to move us toward Him. That's why Scripture rightly says, "The fear
of the LORD is a fountain of life, turning a person from the snares of
death" (Proverbs 14:27 NIV) and "The fear of the LORD is the beginning of wisdom; all those who practice it have a good understanding.
His praise endures forever" (Psalm 111:10).

The Enemy did a spectacular job deceiving Adam and Eve. Satan
is also a created being with a built-in, seared fear capacity, but with an
agenda to rule creation as well. He doesn't create anything that has not
been before—only God does that—so his primary means of working
is to take anything God creates, which is invariably good, and twist it.
Repurpose it, if you will. What God meant to be a tool in our lives to
bring order and to create in us awe, worship, and reverence, the Enemy
uses to send all manner of destruction into our lives.

A Powerful Tool in the Wrong Hands

It reads almost like the riveting plot to an action movie. A weapon
created to ensure peace and protect was hijacked by the Enemy and
meant to destroy and cause chaos. Sweaty palms, eye covering, and
heart pounding are altogether appropriate when we consider the
destruction the Enemy has planned, using the tool of fear against
the children of God. It is important to realize that his motives for

harassing us are altogether evil. Fear results in the following destructive outcomes.

Fear Causes Us to Hide and Shrink Back

When a person feels threatened, a natural reaction is to try to flee from whatever looms large. Self-preservation isn't a bad thing in itself. Imagine how short our life spans would be if we ran headlong into danger whenever we encountered it. I'd never make it home from the grocery store. Likewise, parents wisely make decisions to instill proper fear in their children. We tell them, "No, don't touch that. It's hot!" or warn them of the consequences of reckless and disobedient behavior.

However, when the Enemy threatens us and fear grabs hold, our instinct is to hide from the situation and even from the Lord, as if that were possible. Fear sets us on the run. In light of the persecution of believers on the rise today, even in America, it is easy to be tricked into believing that faith should become a quiet, personal matter. After all, if we, or our children, go public, we will inevitably encounter resistance.

Scripture demonstrates this fight or flight response when Goliath taunted the troops of Israel. For 40 days the Philistine shouted insults and used his towering stature to send them running for the hills. While the army of Israel feared Goliath and shrank back, David feared something greater than Goliath.

> David said to the Philistine, "You come against me with sword and spear and javelin, but I come against you in the name of the LORD Almighty, the God of the armies of Israel, whom you have defied. This day the LORD will deliver you into my hands, and I'll strike you down...and the whole world will know that there is a God in Israel. All those gathered here will know that it is not by sword or spear that the LORD saves; for the battle is the LORD's, and he will give all of you into our hands" (1 Samuel 17:45-47 NIV).

Fear Causes Us to Make Hasty Decisions

We know this is true, don't we? We have seen it play out time and again. Terror causes us to become reactionary, making the wisest decision we can *in the moment*. Consider the last time you saw a squirrel in the road. Its first instinct is to run, but quite often it freezes, and then turns around and heads in the opposite direction. While the first instinct might have led it safely across the path, the second caused it to be run over.

All too often this same reactionary movement does not involve seeking the wisdom of the Lord but capitalizes on our need for control. We scramble until we feel in control of the situation rather than embracing the tension of not having the answer. Remember again that fear is meant to remind us who is in ultimate control and to cause us to seek Him.

Abraham made a decision on the fly that nearly cost him his wife and certainly caused him to lose face in the eyes of a foreign king. Because he was afraid Pharaoh would kill him and take his wife, Abraham lied and told others she was his sister (see Genesis 12 for the whole story). The results were disastrous for everyone. God was angry and people were harmed, not to mention all the distress this must have caused his wife, Sarai. Eight chapters later the whole scene plays out again in almost the same way with King Abimelek. Again, rather than falling on his face before the Lord and waiting there for his next move, Abraham hastily devises his own scheme.

Mamas, let's be quick to take note of this temptation when we face fear. Rather than running to WebMD on the internet, our mothers, our best friends, or even the school board, we would be best served to humble ourselves before the Lord and slow down.

Fear Disorients Us

It might also surprise you to know that built into God's plan for fear is a disorientation of our senses. I think this was meant to assist us in worship, reverence, and awe. But regardless, we see this happen whenever someone in Scripture encounters deity. Isaiah saw a vision of the Lord in Isaiah 6 and was completely undone by what he saw. He heard the voice of the angels. "They were calling to one another: 'Holy, holy, holy is the LORD Almighty; the whole earth is full of his glory'" (Isaiah 6:3 NIV). Everything around him shook, the temple was filled with smoke, and Isaiah declared himself wrecked before God Almighty.

Daniel faced a similar situation when he saw a man who was probably a vision of the preincarnate Christ hovering above the water on a walk to wash up (see Daniel 10). The men with him were overwhelmed with such fear that they ran and hid (see fear reaction number 1) while Daniel fell facedown. Daniel tells us, "I was left alone, gazing at this great vision; I had no strength left, my face turned deathly pale and I was helpless. Then I heard him speaking, and as I listened to him, I fell into a deep sleep, my face to the ground. A hand touched me and set me trembling on my hands and knees" (Daniel 10:8-10 NIV). Talk about sensory overload.

It would be so tempting to believe this overwhelming undoing is only a perversion of the tool of fear, but we would be wrong. God fully intends to move us from disorientation into peace as we trust in Him. As we surrender fear into the hands of God, what will overcome is peace. It may not be easy, and it may be a hard-fought battle for us as we cling to Him, but as we still ourselves in awe of Him, He will strengthen us.

> While he was saying this to me, I bowed with my face toward the ground and was speechless. Then one who looked like a man touched my lips, and I opened my mouth and began to speak. I said to the one standing before me, "I am overcome with anguish because of the vision, my lord, and I feel very weak. How can I, your servant, talk with you, my lord? My strength is gone and I can hardly breathe."

> Again the one who looked like a man touched me and gave me strength. "Do not be afraid, you who are highly esteemed," he said. "Peace! Be strong now; be strong."
>
> When he spoke to me, I was strengthened and said, "Speak, my lord, since you have given me strength" (Daniel 10:15-19 NIV).

Physiologically, the reaction to anxiety and the reason we become disoriented when we feel afraid makes sense. Our bodies shut down some of the prefrontal cortex of our brains when we feel anxious. It is biologically correct to say that when we are afraid we can't think straight.[2] God created our brains. Did we expect less?

You might also find it encouraging to know that God uses the disorienting side of fear to slay our enemies. First Samuel 14 tells about the impending attack of the Philistine enemy army on the children of Israel. "Panic struck the whole army—those in the camp and field, and those in the outposts and raiding parties—and the ground shook. It was a panic sent by God" (1 Samuel 14:15 NIV). The result is almost unbelievable, even comical. "Then Saul and all his men assembled and went to the battle. They found the Philistines in total confusion, striking each other with their swords...So on that day the LORD saved Israel, and the battle moved on beyond Beth Aven" (1 Samuel 14:20,23 NIV).

Fear Makes Disobedience Seem Permissible

One of our favorite things to do as a family is travel. The kids carry their own backpacks, know how to pack bags, and enjoy public transportation. My city of choice is Chicago, and we usually make it there a couple of times a year for a weekend of museums, parks, and deep-dish pizza.

One of my daughters struggles with sensory issues that make certain sounds and certain transitions difficult. Most of the time she deals with this sensitivity with very little assistance and manages the minor stresses well. But on a recent trip to Chicago, when we were getting on a train and everyone else hopped on without a problem, my daughter hesitated. She was frozen by the people and the sounds and the knowledge that she could mess up this transition or lose her people. Mike and I didn't anticipate the delay, and because of the crowd we were in a hurry. "Honey, go! We need to move forward. Go! Get on!" I pled. But she was so filled with fear that she couldn't move.

My daughter's tendency to become "stuck" when she's afraid is such a poignant reminder to me of our tendency, as children of God, to feel as though our fear makes disobedience acceptable, even rational. As a parent, I don't always know the origin of her fears or when they will pop up next, but as a mother who loves her, I don't always remove or cater to her fears. There would be no limit to what we would be forced to avoid. Patiently and with thought for her capacity, I ask and require her to obey me when I give her direction. I always want to know when she feels afraid, but I won't always change the directions I give her. Sometimes I simply have more information than she does.

Likewise, the Father knows what we are made of and what trips us up. If He were to cater to our wishes for an anxiety-free existence, we would not grow. "The testing of your faith produces steadfastness," says James 1:3. This may not come as a huge revelation to you, but even when we feel afraid, our God expects us to obey Him.

After the children of Israel left captivity in Egypt under Moses's direction, they spent time in the wilderness, getting ready to enter the promised land. The Lord explicitly told them the land where they were headed was occupied by enemies of several nationalities. He would send an angel with them, whom He expected them to obey.

> If you carefully obey his voice and do all that I say, then I will be an enemy to your enemies and an adversary to your adversaries...I will not drive them out from before you in one year, lest the land become desolate and the wild beasts

> multiply against you. Little by little I will drive them out
> from before you, until you have increased and possessed
> the land (Exodus 23:22,29-30).

This generation of Israelites were the ones who crossed the Red
Sea. They were the ones who had seen the plagues in Egypt, experienced Passover, and walked on dry ground through a body of water,
only to see it close on Pharaoh's army. They had lived on a supernatural food that fell every morning the whole 40 years they were in the
desert. The generation I call the Red Sea Generation had undoubtedly
experienced God's mercy and provision. So when God asked them to
send 12 spies into the promised land to bring a report back to the people before they entered, the question before the spies was not *if* they
would be headed into the land, but *when*.

When the spies returned to the congregation of people after their
40-day survey of the promised land, they entered camp with a sam-
ple of the choice fruits awaiting them. The reports of their goodness
were unanimous, because of course the land God said He was giving
them would be good. He is a good Father. He gives good gifts. The
reports of the land flowing with milk and honey must have made the
people salivate. They had been living on manna, meat, and water for
a year and a half already. However, the report also included a brief-
ing on the occupants in the land. Their cities were fortified and their
people strong.

Caleb, in complete belief, says, "Let us go up at once and occupy
it, for we are well able to overcome it" (Numbers 13:30). I so want to
have that response when something bewildering comes my way. My
friend Annie often reminds me that the people in Scripture didn't
know the ending to the story. They didn't have the pleasure of flip-
ping a few chapters and seeing their happy endings. They operated
the same way we do, based on the evidence and circumstances right in
front of us. Ten of the other spies changed their tune about the land.
Instead of focusing on its goodness and the faithfulness of God, they

fixated on the fear and risk ahead. "The land, through which we have gone to spy it out, is a land that devours its inhabitants, and all the people that we saw in it are of great height...and we seemed to ourselves like grasshoppers, and so we seemed to them" (verses 32-33).

At this point I have to shake my head. The Red Sea Generation had already been through so much with God. He had already proved so faithful. Why the sudden doubt? If I am honest, however, I must admit I find myself and my temptation carried away by the fear in their response. "Why is the LORD bringing us into this land, to fall by the sword? Our wives and our little ones will become a prey. Would it not be better for us to go back to Egypt?" (Numbers 14:3). They were afraid. They didn't want to put everyone's lives on the line, especially when *everyone* included their children. This fear, this risk, made even captivity look like the best option available.

I'm choking even as I write these words. I know this temptation to choose to believe that I could somehow find a better way through a trial than the route the Lord has laid before me. I often choose to believe what I see with my eyes and feel in my quaking emotions rather than to walk forward in faith. As the writer of Hebrews reminds us, however, "Faith is the substance of things hoped for, the evidence of things not seen" (Hebrews 11:1 KJV).

> Your fear does not negate your responsibility to obey the Lord.

Faith is the *substance*. It's the stuff we must hold on to and wrestle down when emotions and perhaps the Enemy try to persuade us there is no way to obey. Ten out of 12 spies and a whole lot of fear persuaded the Israelites that what lay ahead of them was a greater reality than the promise of God's presence and power with them. They went so far as to try to choose another leader instead of the one God had appointed (Moses) and head back to Egypt. The consequences were dire. God called their fear and refusal to move forward an act of disobedience.

Ultimately, only the two spies, Caleb and Joshua, and the children of the Red Sea Generation entered the land. The rest faced wandering and death in a desert.

I want to reiterate this. Your fear does not negate your responsibility to obey the Lord. Not even if your giants make you look like a grasshopper.

Fear Enslaves Us

> Fear of man will prove to be a snare, but whoever trusts in the Lord is kept safe (Proverbs 29:25 NIV).

Anxiety. Depression. The stress of fear takes a toll on our bodies. At one point in my journey, I was stuck in such a cycle of fear that the mere thought of a certain situation caused my stomach and guts to revolt. I mean sick, sick. When we allow fear to capture our minds. we forfeit the peace God longs for His children to experience and enjoy. In a sense we are bound and shackled to things we fear. We may not feel the weight of the shackles, but as we spin to self-preserve we become wearier and wearier.

Even now I'm considering the ways fear has held me bound. The coming dawn of the new millennium, excitingly called Y2K, found me stocking up on candles and batteries. Several years back I spent my summer preoccupied with canning and preserving food "just in case." I'm not talking about preserving out of good stewardship; I was serving fear that told me we might not have enough if something happened. It drove my thought processes for an entire summer. I've dragged my feet to have medical procedures done because I was afraid of the aftermath. And as I write, my mind is flickering to a nebulizer I've stored in my closet since 2005 just in case my kids need it and we can't get one.

All that might not seem outlandish to you. (I'm sure others of you think I'm a fruitcake.) Some of the steps I took to self-preserve were probably prudent for a while, but as I look closely at the common denominator, I know I continue to face an undercurrent of fear that I might be unable to provide for my family or take care of myself. That's the hook right there. The thing the Lord continues to show me over and over is that fear in anything but Him grows and takes me places and keeps me places where I don't want to be. Further, the decisions I make based in fear only bear bad fruit.

> I sought the LORD, and he answered me and *delivered* me from all my fears (Psalm 34:4, emphasis added).

I'm learning not to resent fear, but rather to use it as an indicator light. Much like the oil light in my car, or the one that looks like a squiggly carburetor or something, fear flashing in me has meaning. It is, after all, a God-given emotion and can even become a tool if we discipline our hearts to respond correctly. In the hands of the Lord, fear produces in us reverence and worship and helps us set healthy boundaries. In the grip of the Enemy, fear burns us like a crazy, roaring wildfire.

Jesus sets us straight about the antidote to dangerous fear.

> I will warn you whom to fear: fear him (Luke 12:5).

Lord,

I see places in my life where dangerous roots of fear have grabbed hold. I know, as it says in 1 John 4:18, that "there is no fear in love, but perfect love casts out fear." Will You begin revealing to me places in my life and in my mothering where my fear is leading me to sin? Forgive and heal in me that place where I shrink back and hide rather than walking in faith that You will protect me. Forgive me for the times I make hasty decisions without seeking You first. Help me when the anxiety and fear become disorienting and consuming. I desire to walk in freedom from the bondage of fear. Thank You that You know the way of my family, the path ahead, and that You still say, "Do not fear." I choose to trust You today. In Jesus's name, amen.

4

The Fumbled Torch

Everybody has a chapter they don't read out loud.
—STEVE MARABOLI

I love the Olympics. At some indescribable level, I find myself fascinated with the whole event. There is just something so poignant and moving about watching athletes who have trained year upon year participate. They represent and compete on behalf of countries around the world who have set aside differences to come together in the name of good-natured competition. I love every day of the competition and try not to miss any of the good sports (gymnastics, swimming, track and field, anyone?). Nothing, however, is more poignant to me than the opening ceremonies.

Just so you know the full depth of this Olympic love, I present two outrageous illustrations. The first was shortly after our daughter came home from Guatemala. Becoming a mother of two was a completely bewildering experience, and like most mothers I found myself exhausted and drained. The night of the 2006 Winter Olympic opening games ceremony, my husband asked if we could find a babysitter and go out for dinner. At that stage of the game any break was a good break, and I enjoyed a good meal and time alone with Mike.

At the restaurant he informed me he had made a reservation for me at a hotel nearby and that he had a suitcase packed in the car for a night away. He'd be dropping me off on our way home so I could watch the opening ceremony in peace. That act of love still nearly does me in.

The second illustration was during the 2012 Summer Olympics. I ordered a satellite dish, breaking a two-year television-free streak in our home. But then to complicate matters, dear friends asked all four of our children to be in their wedding the night of the opening ceremony. I was floored at the tragedy of the timing, but not to be deterred, I bought a DVR package to make sure we could at least watch when we arrived home.

Ridiculousness aside, my favorite part of the ceremony is the passing of the Olympic flame from torch to torch. The flame travels from Greece, its point of origin, to the location of the games. The flame has flown on airplanes and traveled by boat and has been on almost every continent. It is handed from person to person, average Joe to celebrity, war heroes to retired athletes, politicians to workers, all the way to the site of the Olympics.

While I'm not an expert, three steps to an Olympic flame handoff are absolutely clear in my mind. Step one involves the original runner entering the exchange zone. Step two is the moment when the handoff occurs. In this moment, both runners hold the torch. In step three, the original runner lets go and the second runner begins running toward the destination.

Just like the flame, faith was designed to be passed from generation to generation until Christ returns. Each generation receives the blessings won by the previous generation, but it also faces the trials, mistakes, and consequences born of its failure. Handoffs are tricky things, no matter the baggage of the past. God has clearly communicated to His children, however, that faith flows best downhill, from parent to child. Moses told the children of Israel,

> These are the commands, decrees and laws the LORD your
> God directed me to teach you to observe in the land that

you are crossing the Jordan to possess, so that you, your children and their children after them may fear the LORD your God as long as you live by keeping all his decrees and commands that I give you, and so that you may enjoy long life...Impress them on your children. Talk about them when you sit at home and when you walk along the road, when you lie down and when you get up (Deuteronomy 6:1-2,7 NIV).

Obey and teach your kids to obey so they can teach their kids to obey. Make it your job. Occupy yourself with it. The responsibility is staggering. Consider the words of the psalmist:

Things we have heard and known, things our ancestors have told us. We will not hide them from their descendants; we will tell the next generation the praiseworthy deeds of the LORD, his power, and the wonders he has done. He decreed statutes for Jacob and established the law in Israel, which he commanded our ancestors to teach their children, so the next generation would know them, even the children yet to be born, and they in turn would tell their children. Then they would put their trust in God and would not forget his deeds but would keep his commands (Psalm 78:3-7 NIV).

A Rotten Example

God commands His children to teach their offspring who He is and what He has done so they will put their trust in Him. However, if you are like me or countless other believers like me, the handoff of faith was not seamless. Everyday life confirms what we already know to be true—the torch sometimes falls to the ground. Someone I love dearly reminds me regularly that she didn't have an example in her parents. They were divorced when she was young and they are better examples for what not to do than examples to emulate. "No one taught me how to do this Christian mothering stuff. I didn't have an example. I don't know what I'm doing."

It's so tempting to believe we can sideline ourselves from a lack of modeling. Yet blessed few of us had perfect role models. If your parents did it all wrong, you are in terrific company.

Scripture is filled with case after case of faith-torch drops and the children who lean over and pick them up and begin running again. As the Red Sea Generation died off in the wilderness, their children grew and prepared to enter the promised land. This generation would be the one to cross over the Jordan River into the land God promised them. The Hebrew word for "cross over" is *abar*. Those who crossed over, or the Abar Generation, if you will, were well acquainted with the discipline of God. We also call them the Grave Digger Generation, because they buried an average of 85 bodies a day over the course of the 40 years in the wilderness. Isn't that wild? Eighty-five funerals were required each day while the disbelieving and disobedient Red Sea Generation died as a consequence of their sin.

The thought haunts me. Imagine watching the parents you love prepare for their inevitable deaths as all the adults you know begin to perish. The Abars, at the very oldest, would have been 59 years old (19 at the time of the rebellion, plus 40 years in the wilderness). They could have remained on the outside of that land and shrugged their shoulders, kicked the dust at their feet, and cited poor heritage for their reason to delay obedience. But they didn't. They prepared for what lay ahead, knowing that although battles would come and they had not seen courageous faith lived out before them, they would move forward anyway. Their response to Joshua's direction to move forward is crystal clear: "All that you have commanded us we will do, and wherever you send us we will go" (Joshua 1:16).

Gideon is also a prime candidate for the lack of role model argument. When God called him to deliver the Israelites from the Midianites, his father was a Baal worshiper. Not just a whimsical testing-the-water worshiper, either. His father, Joash, had built an altar to

Baal and an Asherah pole beside it. Gideon and Joash were up to their necks in false worship when the angel of God appeared and called Gideon a mighty warrior who would save Israel.

Like us, Gideon faltered. "'Pardon me, my lord,' Gideon replied, 'but how can I save Israel? My clan is the weakest in Manasseh, and I am the least in my family'" (Judges 6:15 NIV). Poor Gideon's first assignment from God in delivering the children of Israel was to confront the idols in his family of origin, specifically tearing them down and rebuilding an altar to the Lord.

Gideon was terrified.

> Gideon took ten of his servants and did as the LORD told him. But because he was afraid of his family and the townspeople, he did it at night rather than in the daytime. In the morning when the people of the town got up, there was Baal's altar, demolished, with the Asherah pole beside it cut down and the second bull sacrificed on the newly built altar! (Judges 6:27-28 NIV).

What moved Gideon from familial excuses and fear to faith? The answer to that question is the promise of God's presence with him as he went. "The LORD answered, 'I will be with you, and you will strike down all the Midianites, leaving none alive'" (Judges 6:16 NIV). God's promised presence with us enables us to overcome any setback our family of origin dealt us. We are not expected to figure out this journey alone; He doesn't even want us to try.

This isn't simply a theory. God does change generations after the absolute failure of one. My friend Erin's stepfather victimized her sexually and emotionally from the time she was a young age. While still in her teens, she became pregnant with his child and chose to place the baby for adoption. Perhaps equally devastating is that this man claimed to be a pastor and led a small, deceived flock. Erin faced unspeakable obstacles to discovering true, life-giving faith. The choice to break free from the abuse and perversion of her past and reach toward the healing Christ alone can bring transformed her. She is now a happy, joyful, and healing wife and young mother. I have never heard Erin use her upbringing as an excuse to fall down on her task of raising her own beautiful children. Quite the contrary, her love for the Lord is contagious and her redemption and walk with Christ spur on all who know her story.[1]

An Ugly Track Record

Family failings aren't the only excuse for clumsy handoffs of faith to our children. Many of us believe we have done something to disqualify us from passing on the righteous standard God sets for believers. More than once I have been tempted to believe I have no business setting a standard for my children that I didn't keep myself. Shame and guilt can bind us up until we shut up, and I think that is exactly what the enemy of our souls has planned.

Society isn't helping parents in this arena. Others pounce on an ounce of something that appears hypocritical. It almost appears that society leans forward to watch for the failure of those who call themselves Christian, as though that designation implies perfection. This happens to politicians, business people, those in ministry, and almost anyone in the public eye. Immorality? Front page news. While our faith should define and shape our actions, it's impossible to meet a standard of perfection. It should not catch us off guard that the world is watching for us to fail. Satan himself is called the accuser of the brothers (Revelation 12:10) and he persists in his accusation and waits for our humiliation to discredit our walk with Christ. After all, if Satan can't have our allegiance, he'll stop at nothing to destroy our influence. The world follows suit.

It is tempting to stare hard at our weaknesses and areas of temptation and disqualify ourselves from leading spiritually in those areas. The error in becoming stuck in this thinking is twofold. First, we don't set the standard; God does. Believing I have done something that has disqualified me from leading my children wrongly makes *my* behavior, values, and decisions the standard rather than God's righteous ways. His expectations for my children to love and obey Him are not placed on a sliding scale, based on the performance of the rest of the class or that of their parents. His expectations remain unchanging, and that is fantastic news for us. We call this the doctrine of immutability. It's a heavy, theological word that I beg you to use in your next game of Scrabble, and it means God does not change. He is, in His very essence, changeless. God says of Himself, "For I the LORD do not change; therefore you, O children of Jacob, are not consumed" (Malachi 3:6). If God had a scale that slid, we would need to be fearful about the measuring stick He would use to measure us. The standard God uses is perfection. All sin, whether measured with a teaspoon or an ocean, is enough to sever relationship with Him.

Romans 6:23 tells us "the wages of sin is death." God's righteous standard has never bent and it will never bend to let people into right relationship or into eternity. God's penalty for sin was paid in full for you and for me and for our children when Jesus died in our place on the cross. Truly, God's immutability is precious because He decided His anger toward sin would be satisfied completely by Jesus's death—and He cannot and will not change His mind.

This means that, as a parent, my performance or lack thereof does not adjust the standard. I think the Enemy would love nothing more than for me to lower or adjust the guidelines for righteous living God has set for my family.

The second reason my past does not disqualify me is that failure on my part to meet that standard has already been covered in full by Jesus. He expects my obedience as a demonstration of my love for Him. The same is true for my children. It is my job to point my children to Jesus and help them understand they have a Father who desires a right relationship with them.

One area where shame and guilt are having a field day is dating and sexual purity. Mothers and fathers who were sexually active before they married can easily become convinced that encouraging their children to practice abstinence and to guard their hearts makes them hypocrites. "I'm not one to talk, because when I was their age..." seems to be the thinking. If I give this line of thinking an inch of room, it will have plenty of kindling to burn like a wildfire inside me. I was boy crazy from the age of five and did not truly obey Jesus until I was 17. By that time, my heart had not only been left unguarded, it was torn deeply and covered in calluses. *But Jesus.* When Jesus tenderly drew me, He began the process of reviving and repairing. A great deal of time was spent in repentance before Him, because I needed to agree with Him that I'd made a lot of poor choices. He has sweetly tended my heart until it has become strong again, healed with scars. In some ways, those scars have empowered me with greater faith to teach my children that God's way is always the best way.

My friends Jeremy and Rhonda fell in love young. Rhonda told me the first time she saw Jeremy she was 15 years old and he was working as a bag boy in a grocery store. She turned and told her mom she was going to marry Jeremy, and from that time forward she was set on winning her guy. They both were from unbelieving and dysfunctional homes. Rhonda was 19 when she got pregnant with their first child, and two years later she gave birth to their second. And then they decided to get married.

They ran with a fast crowd and were barely adults themselves when they found themselves with a family. On one occasion they separated for a few months, trying to decide if marriage was what they really wanted. It wasn't until their 16-year-old daughter, Becca, began begging her mom to attend church with her that things began to change. Shortly thereafter, Jeremy and Rhonda gave their lives to Jesus and life turned upside down.

It was not an easy ride. History repeated itself as generational patterns began to rear up in their daughter. She ran away from home to be with her boyfriend and scared her poor, newly believing parents half to death. Instead of excusing her behavior, or simply remaining angry, they leaned into the Holy Spirit and sought wisdom for how to shepherd their wayward child.

I've watched Jeremy and Rhonda up close for years now and have seen how God has changed them. Their two oldest were raised on the rocky path, but they have the new legacy of two parents who are completely seeking the Lord and His will for their lives. These two are now dynamic soul winners. They leverage their past, allowing their broken story to be useful in helping them reach lost people, not the least of which have been both of Rhonda's parents and her brother. Jeremy and Rhonda are heroes with pasts. Some of the greatest heroes are.

"I Don't Know How"

When God hands you a difficult assignment, it seems to be a natural reaction to throw your hands up and express disillusionment and confusion. This is certainly the truth in motherhood, isn't it? "I don't know how I'm ever going to get any sleep." "I don't know when to introduce solid food." "I don't know how to teach them to listen to me." "How will they come to know Jesus?" "Am I doing enough?" "Am I doing too much?" "How do I communicate with my daughter when she is totally hormonal and seems to have lost her mind?"

I can't be the only one asking questions like these. Friend, what are your questions in this season of your parenting journey? What is keeping you up at night, longing for answers?

If we were to sit knee to knee, I'd rattle off a list of questions I wish I knew the answers to and things I don't know how to do where my children are concerned. And when I don't know how to do something, I tend to stay frozen in place. This subtle quirk has proven to be a detriment in so many areas of life. Don't know what to cook for dinner? Might as well put it off. (News flash, folks, dinner has never once cooked itself, and procrastinating doesn't make it easier.) Parenting children to know, love, and follow Christ is not a well-worn path for me. It would be so easy to remain stuck in "I don't know how" and freeze. The problem is my kids won't stop growing and there is no time for delay. Now is my season for child-rearing. This is my leg of the race.

Based on the authority of the Word of God, I can say to you clearly that God knows you can't do this on your own. He doesn't even want you to try. We easily overlook Bible passages familiar to us in our faith walk and fail to apply them to our mothering. But consider the following passages afresh, reflecting on your "I don't knows" of motherhood.

- "Trust in the LORD with all your heart, and do not lean on your own understanding. In all your ways acknowledge him, and he will make straight your paths" (Proverbs 3:5-6).
- "If any of you lacks wisdom, you should ask God, who gives generously to all without finding fault, and it will be given to you" (James 1:5 NIV).
- "But he said to me, 'My grace is sufficient for you, for my power is made perfect in weakness.' Therefore I will boast all the more gladly of my weaknesses, so that the power of Christ may rest upon me" (2 Corinthians 12:9).

Are you ready to throw up your hands and acknowledge you don't know how to do everything you think a mother should and that you desperately need wisdom? The sooner we realize we don't have the answers, that we don't know how this will turn out, and that we need help, the closer we get to the answers we need. Great news: God is like a magnet to those who need Him.

Run On

On a cold, drizzly day in Vancouver, British Columbia, a crowd was gathered to cheer as runners jogged by carrying the Olympic flame. Everyone was wearing layers of clothing, ponchos, and holding umbrellas as the runner with the lit torch ran into view. The pavement was wet and this runner and the next one paused to pass the flame. The second runner's torch lit and the crowd cheered wildly in the background. They did a little dance, interlocking arms and circling with both torches lit, and then it happened. The second torch, the one the second runner was supposed to depart with, fell to the soggy ground.

The crowd literally gasped and both runners froze and stared at the ground. That's when a coach from the crowd walked over, leaned down, and picked up the torch. He put his arm around the next runner and whispered something in her ear. Then holding the torch, she took off running.[2]

I so wish I knew what he said in that moment. Can we level for a minute? I don't know how you came to this place in this journey with me and the Lord. I don't know if you came in running strong like a champion, faith all ablaze, strides nice and long. Or if you've been running and trying, but you are so tired, and you feel as though your torch is lying on the ground. Either way, may I whisper something in your ear?

Jesus is with you, mighty warrior. This is your leg of the race. Run on, mama. Run on.

Lord,

I don't know how this is going to all turn out, but I do know I need You for every part of the journey ahead. Forgive me for worrying and blaming rather than bringing my needs and concerns to You. It's reassuring to know there is not a moment of my story that You don't know or can't overcome. Thank You for the forgiveness You offer me through Jesus and the fresh start we can make right now. I want You to be the center of our family and raising Christ followers to be my aim. Step in now as I yield. I need You. In Jesus's name I pray, amen.

5

The Beautiful Surrender

*Courage is a special kind of knowledge: the knowledge
of how to fear what ought to be feared and how
not to fear what ought not to be feared.*
—David Ben-Gurion

If it's going to be a struggle, I'm going down fighting. Surrender seems like a bad idea. Failing to give something your all is almost like sacrilege, because somehow, someway, I've come to believe that if I try hard enough, put in enough hours, practice, scrape my knees and get up again, and give blood, sweat, and tears, I'm going to be able to find mastery. Generally, this has been beneficial in my walk with the Lord and in life in general, but a few times I've realized God Himself was on the other side of the tug-of-war I was playing.

God on the Other Side of the Rope

Fear had gained a foothold in my life.

How did that happen?

How did I get here?

Giants, of course, aren't born giants. Goliath wasn't born nine feet tall—he began life as an infant. So it was with the fear in my life. It crept in, in subtleties, but gradually it grew into a complete preoccupation of my mind. I eventually found myself sitting on the sofa of a wonderful, godly counselor. As we talked, I described the darkness I felt to her. I explained how I had been trying so hard to raise a godly family. She nodded as I described trying to find a balance between ministry and being a mother. I cried and explained that I trusted God and loved Him and knew in my head that He had us, but for some reason my heart was quaking anyway. What if God used my kids to do the hard things I had been praying for?

She leaned over and asked in a gentle, uncondemning tone, "Lee, do you think you have made an idol out of your children?"

My heart reeled. She was right. I had not built an image of another god to worship, but I was exchanging the promises of God's peace and presence for a fixation.

John Calvin said, "The evil in our desire typically does not lie in what we want, but that we want it too much." In one of my favorite Bible studies, *No Other Gods,* Kelly Minter explains it may be difficult to decide if something has become an idol to us, because at first glance (or ten, twelve, or a thousand glances) it might not seem like a bad thing. She introduced me to the idea of "functional gods." She says, "I especially like the use of this phrase because sometimes it's easier for me to determine what functions for me as a god as opposed to what is false."[1]

What was haunting about my counselor's words was that I knew, in an instant, that they were right. I had idolized a perfect family where I provided my kids with the safety and security I hadn't always felt growing up. My parents divorced when I was 11, and in my mind I've created an image of what a godly family looks like. It looks like a mother who is home in the mornings and makes her kids hot breakfasts. It looks like leading my kids in devotions at the breakfast table every morning. It looks like being active in their classrooms and sports activities, and providing the place all their friends want to hang out. I've gone to great lengths to be a godly wife who does the laundry, cooking, cleaning, and—forgive my bluntness—is a bedroom diva for her man. I wanted to be home when the kids got home from school with chocolate chip cookies ready and have home-cooked meals waiting when Mike got home each evening. I wanted our tribe to say, "My mom loves me. I loved my childhood."

Truly, all that is not that far off course. Don't we all want our kids to have a happy childhood? What I am coming to realize, though, is that although my heart has been set on something fantastic, it is a by-product of what *may* happen as I seek Him. This isn't truly worshiping God and placing my will in His hands.

Testing, Testing

Periodically, the Lord lifts the veil on a passage of Scripture you may have read dozens of times before. It becomes alive and takes on new meaning because of the moment in time you have entered. Genesis 22 is one of those passages for me. I imagine it begins on an average day, when Abraham is busy around the house. Sarah probably had him working on a honey-do list a mile long, or maybe he was out in the field supervising his shepherds. We can picture him doing normal family things when God began testing him. I circled the word *test* in orange in my Bible because it occurred to me that Scripture tells us what this is about before we even read the rest. That comforts me, too, because the test itself is awful.

> [God] said to him, "Abraham!"
> And he said, "Here I am."
> He said, "Take your son, your only son Isaac, whom you love, and go to the land of Moriah, and offer him there as a burnt offering on one of the mountains of which I shall tell you" (Genesis 22:1-2).

This is the God Abraham left his country and his people to obey and follow. I probably would have expected the Lord to give me a pass on any further tests. But when God whispered this command, imagine how Abraham must have experienced all the emotions any other parent would. Shock, disbelief, and absolute dread would be my feelings. I'm sure they were Abraham's feelings as well, because he loved Isaac deeply. God makes sure we know that, too, because he reiterates it. "Take your son, your only son Isaac, whom you love" (verse 2).

I missed that before—this precious tenderness of God, when He acknowledges the deep places in Abraham's heart where he loves his son so very much. God remembered the work it took to get Isaac. I mean, countless decades of trying to conceive. (And I thought two years was a long time.) God knows how much we love these kids and how much we want what we think is best for them.

Abraham got up early the next morning and set out to obey the Lord. He probably kissed Sarah's cheek as he said good-bye, but we have zero record of him telling her what was about to happen or what the Lord had asked him to do. (I find that understandable.) He gathered up Isaac, not understanding in the least what God was doing, but obeying anyway.

As the two traveled, Isaac probably snacked along the way because they were, after all, road-tripping. My guess is Abraham could hardly talk because of the lump in his throat. They got to the spot and he built the altar and bound his son.

Don't sugarcoat this in your mind. Let it make your guts reel. He had raised the knife to slay his son when God called out, "Abraham, Abraham!"

He said, "Here I am."

God told him, "Do not lay your hand on the boy or do anything to him, for now I know that you fear God, seeing you have not withheld your son, your only son, from me" (Genesis 22:12). Scripture tells us Abraham lifts his eyes, sees a ram stuck in the bushes, and offers it as a burnt offering instead of his son, Isaac. Again God calls to him: "Because you have done this and have not withheld your son, your only son, I will surely bless you" (Genesis 22:16-17).

Friends, God knows the depth of love we have for our children. Look at the three instances when God says, "Your son, your only son." God knew exactly what He was asking. He was trying to decide if Abraham's strong love and desire to protect his child would override his obedience when God asked him to let go. This was an idol test if there ever was one. Abraham didn't make little statues of Isaac to worship, but he could very well have made this child, his only son with his wife, Sarah, a functional idol.

We face the temptation to make idols out of our children, along with their happiness and success. We idolize other families and the path the Lord is taking them down. We may even bow to the idols of financial security, health, and safety. Most of those things are crazy good, but we can know for certain that God wants to make sure that He, even before our families, is first in our hearts.

Here's the good news about this kind of test.

1. God knows the depth of our sacrifice and surrender.
2. When God tests he also provides.

That ram caught in the thicket causes Abraham to name that place on Mount Moriah "The Lord will provide" (verse 14). Abraham didn't know the irony or power in the words he had spoken. They were a foreshadow of the complete sacrifice the Father would provide through the death of His own Son, Jesus. For God the Father, there would be no ram in the thicket. He would offer His Son, the Lamb of God, in exchange for the sin of man.

We can know, dear ones, that when God asks us to surrender or sacrifice something, He will provide the strength and means to do it.

A Crazy Proposal

Adoniram Judson was a man whose heart belonged to the Lord. He was smart, handsome, and came from a godly family. He graduated at the top of his class from Brown University, and though he had waited until college to surrender his heart to Christ, when he gave it over there was no holding back. He attended seminary and felt God's call to serve abroad in foreign missions, to preach Christ where He had not yet been named.

Sounds like the kind of guy I'd love to find for my daughter. Great in-laws (because heaven knows, you marry a family), passionate, driven, godly...Who could ask for more? I'm sure Ann Hasseltine's parents felt similarly when their daughter first began mentioning his name around the house. When their relationship started to move more quickly, however, and the driven young Adoniram approached them a short month after their meeting for Ann's hand in marriage, I'm sure the shine of his suitor attire began to dull. Really, one month? The following is the letter he penned. Try to imagine your response as Ann's mother. It shouldn't be too big a stretch.

> I have now to ask, whether you can consent to part with your daughter early next spring, to see her no more in this world; whether you can consent to her departure, and her subjection to the hardships and sufferings of missionary life; whether you can consent to her exposure to the dangers of the ocean, to the fatal influence of the southern climate of India; to every kind of want and distress; to degradation, insult, persecution, and perhaps a violent death. Can you consent to all this, for the sake of him who left his heavenly home, and died for her and for you; for the sake of perishing, immortal souls; for the sake of Zion, and the glory of God? Can you consent to all this, in hope of soon meeting your daughter in the world of glory, with the crown of righteousness, brightened with the acclamations of praise which shall redound to her Savior from heathens saved, through her means, from eternal woe and despair?[2]

Is your heart in your throat too? I think I'd answer, *I'm sorry, dear Adoniram. We really liked you, and you have a lot going for you, but we do not consent. Have you ever considered pastoring locally?*

No, seriously. How would you respond? Ann's father wisely left the decision to her to follow as she felt the Lord leading.

In 1812, 12 days after they were married, Adoniram and Ann Judson set sail for India en route to Burma, becoming America's first foreign missionaries. Adoniram's words were prophetic in nature, as suffering would be the assignment God had for these chosen servants. They are true heroes of the faith, loving Jesus more than they loved this life, sharing Christ even when it hurt.

I'm not sure whom I admire more—the young Judsons or Ann's parents. Everything in me wants to say I believe Christ is worth laying down my life. But laying down my child? Oh, God, for the grace to trust You.

> We are often hindered from giving up our treasures to the Lord out of fear for their safety; this is especially true when those treasures are loved relatives and friends. But we need have no such fears. Our Lord came not to destroy but to save. Everything is safe which we commit to Him, and nothing is really safe which is not so committed.
>
> —A. W. Tozer

Entrust

In Christendom we toss around this phrase casually: "I *surrendered* that to God." We sing it in songs all the time. When we say we surrender something to Christ, we mean we are turning it over to Him. We've decided to quit fighting and we recognize His authority over us. I love that powerful idea, but I was absolutely floored when I began studying and found that Scripture doesn't use that word to describe the process we're talking about. The use of the word *surrender* in Hebrew is strictly applicable for surrendering to another man, as in troop to troop after a battle. In no instance is the word used in relation to what man does toward God. Don't get me wrong, though— the idea is there. Scripture uses other words to describe what man does when overcome with the realization that God is infinitely more powerful and worthy than he is. It uses words like *submit, succumb, self-denial, yield, commit,* and my favorite, *entrust.*

This is such a relief to me. We're not in a battle with God, and we don't need to quit fighting Him. Besides, the warrior mom instinct inside us is alive and strong, and there will be no giving up when it comes to protecting and defending our children. The word *surrender* just doesn't seem to apply. But oh, the blessing of entrusting.

Nothing in this word smacks of giving up because the fight is out of you. Entrusting means giving over the responsibility, putting something into another's care or protection. This is what my heart longs for when it's overwhelmed by my inability to keep my children safe, healthy, protected, obedient, and faithful. I desperately desire to assign the responsibility to someone who will not fail at the task. Sometimes I don't even want to entrust my kids to my husband, let alone to their schools or our government. Mike is a terrific father, but he doesn't apply Band-Aids liberally, he pushes when I'd coddle, and he plays "good cop" when I think it is time for "bad cop."

Yet a deep *yes* is in my spirit when I consider the invitation not to surrender my fight but rather entrust my children to someone who cares even more than I do. I believe Jesus came to this same realization. He did not surrender to the Enemy. Not for one second do I believe the fight was taken out of Jesus. But rather,

> When he was reviled, he did not revile in return; when he suffered, he did not threaten, but continued *entrusting* himself to him who judges justly. He himself bore our sins in his body on the tree, that we might die to sin and live to righteousness. By his wounds you have been healed (1 Peter 2:23-24, emphasis added).

Friends, I think we must consider our surrender, our entrusting, with eyes wide open. God does not promise our families perfect health, financial prosperity, worldly success, or even safety in this world. He will not hand us back everything we lay down. Some of the most godly families I know have faced unspeakable loss. Christ shows us, though, that although God may choose suffering for us, we can entrust to Him everything of great worth, knowing He truly empathizes with our pain, knows the depth of the darkness it may cause, and walks with us through it. During our darkest hour, we may find a depth of fellowship with our Savior we would know in no other way. Jesus said, "Blessed are those who mourn, for they shall be comforted" (Matthew 5:4), and in Psalm 34:18 we are promised that it is the Lord Himself who is "near to the brokenhearted and saves the crushed in spirit." He is and always will be with us.

> We are not looking for blind heroism. Heroes of the faith count the cost of their decision and choose to act even when the cost to self is high.

Let's know what we are getting into. We are not looking for blind heroism. Heroes of the faith count the cost of their decision and choose to act even when the cost to self is high.

A Long Time Coming

The act of surrender is both an event and a process. I'm sure you're familiar with the "mountaintop experience" of learning something new or being a part of something powerful. Many times the decisions you make then have a strong emotional element to them. When the experience ends, the process of living out the commitments you have made begins. It is going to take a sustained commitment to see the change take root and hold.

Recently, I've been wanting to lay down some things I can't control. I've wanted to break up with fear in a real and tangible way, and it's time for a formal ceremony. Mike builds me a fire at the campground where we're staying, I kiss the kids, and they go off to bed.

I sit in front of the fire with a notepad on my lap and begin. "Lord," I write, "I'm sorry for never really letting go of the fear. When You are…" I stop. "You are *worthy* of my trust. Your ways are always better. You are good, and You are right even when, with my limited understanding, I can't understand Your plan. You are kind, Lord, and You are loving. You will never act in a way that will harm me without cause and without benefit. You are wise and I trust You."

Tears flow freely down my cheeks as I realize afresh how much I needed this moment. The Spirit keeps bringing to mind all the reasons I can entrust myself, my family, my fears, and my plans to Him. All these things are so much safer in His hands than my own.

My pen flies across that page, filling my heart with faith, and I recognize again that I can trust Him with my fears. I shift and list them. One by one, I write down the fears that have had roots since I was young. Violence. Suffering. Persecution. I unpack the junk, and as I consider the list I see things I know are going to take more time to sift through than just one evening and one ceremony by a fire. But this is my line in the sand; I will not be mastered by my fears any longer. Christ came for freedom, but I have been enslaved by them, and it is time to let go.

With resolve I name those fears—the places of my heart I have somehow believed I could keep safer than my Lord could—and ask for forgiveness. "Lord, I'm sorry. I'm sorry I haven't run to You sooner. I cast these at Your feet now. I entrust my fears to You. I choose to trust in You." Then I crumple that paper, throw it into the fire, and watch it catch and burn. I simply watch, knowing it is done.

A few minutes later, I feel another stirring. It's time to lay my children before Him. I write down my hopes for them. I list the idols of safety and success and a myriad of other things I've been holding out for. I again ask the Lord for forgiveness and tell Him I trust Him with the four precious gifts He has given me.

As I watch the last crumpled paper burn, a verse from Hebrews comes to mind: "God has said, 'Never will I leave you; never will I forsake you.' So we say with confidence, 'The Lord is my helper; I will not be afraid'" (Hebrews 13:5-6 NIV).

 God is my helper. The word *helper* is *ezer* in Hebrew, the same word used to describe Eve when she was created and the word Christ used for the Holy Spirit ("But when the Helper comes, whom I will send you," John 15:26). I sit in awe that the Lord of the universe would have time for me, time to meet me for this ceremony, my line in the sand. Greater still, I am totally convinced He is committed to helping me follow through with my part of this bargain. Although my spirit feels a thousand pounds lighter, the One to whom I have entrusted what is most precious to me is not burdened by those things or by me in the least. Just the thought causes me to worship.

 Tonight I have gazed long at the fire, realizing how much I've needed this moment. It seems only appropriate that the moon is full. Somewhere across the lake people are releasing paper lanterns. As they float slowly across the sky, one after another, I know deep down that the Lord is celebrating with me. Just the two of us tonight in the dark. This moment in time was for me. Everything I let go of tonight has shackled me and chained me down. Not one of those situations on that paper has been resolved, but I know I don't have to carry them. I whisper in my heart, "Freedom."

 It has been a beautiful surrender.

Father,

I'm so grateful that You have experienced the releasing of a child. This means You aren't standing at a distance from this process of entrusting my family to You. You see the places in my heart that long to protect and hold on too tightly. Forgive me for the ways I am allowing fear and doubt to cloud my belief in You. Will You allow Your Spirit to remind me of Your trustworthiness, Your faithfulness, and Your goodness? Teach me to rest in Your stead-fast, unchanging character. You can have my children. I trust You. Amen.

Part Two

The Making of a Hero in Me

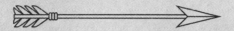

God is in the business of building authentic spiritual leadership. We may be able to talk a good game from the ground while our kids are scaling cliffs in harnesses and helmets, but we will never truly guide them if we never grab hold of the face of the rock and feel the tension on our own muscles. We can buy the gear, we can talk the talk, we can even watch others climb, but until we step out in our own faith walk, this whole effort lacks credibility.

We must disciple our children out of habits being developed in our own lives. Please notice I said being *developed* and not *perfected*. The following five chapters build a framework (and an acronym) for mothers who desire to move forward in faith, believing God will use them to shape the heroes in their homes. We are leaving behind fear and putting on our BRAVE, trusting that God is fully invested in our process and will guide us step by step.

Fear has been laid aside. It's time for BRAVE.

Believe God
Reflect
Ask forgiveness
Vigilantly Pray
Equip Them

6

Believe God

The ancestor of every action is thought.
—Ralph Waldo Emerson

He must have hung his head in exhaustion and disbelief. After all they had been through together, these men and women had picked up rocks to stone him. He could scarcely imagine where the divergence had formed between him and his own people, but clearly they had experienced the miracles and hand of God during the exodus with two very different perspectives. Caleb probably didn't view himself as a hero. He simply was a man who believed God. He didn't just believe in God—any fool could plainly see there was a God after the plagues in Egypt. Caleb believed God Himself, and that He could and would do what He said He would do.

All his peers had lived as slaves in Egypt. Scripture tells us the people of Israel "groaned because of their slavery and cried out for help... God saw the people of Israel—and God knew" (Exodus 2:23,25). God heard them and knew their suffering. He raised up a deliverer, Moses, an unlikely but godly spokesman for both the Lord and His people. Caleb was watching as God brought the superpower of the world, Egypt, to its knees.

This was not a clean, animated rendition like *The Prince of Egypt*.

All the water—the river Nile, the canals, the ponds, pools of water, and even the jars of water in their homes—turned to blood. They were nasty, stinking pots of death. Frogs, gnats, flies, dying livestock, boils, hail, locusts, and finally complete darkness overtook Egypt. God was moving on behalf of His suffering people. When the night of Passover came, Caleb's people took the blood of a lamb and painted it over the doorposts of their home as the Lord told Moses they should do. That night the Lord passed through and took the life of every first-born Egyptian and brought His people out of the land. It wasn't a simple deliverance; it was complicated, it was sensory, and it was strong. God caused them to leave slavery as victors with prizes—their Egyptian neighbors shoved silver, gold, jewelry, and clothing into their hands as they left.

These events were fresh in Caleb's mind as he considered the days following the exodus when Moses stood to remind the people, "Remember this day in which you came out from Egypt, out of the house of slavery, for by a strong hand the LORD brought you out from this place...You shall tell your son [on the day you celebrate Passover in the promised land], 'It is because of what the LORD did for me when I came out of Egypt'...For with a strong hand the LORD has brought you out" (Exodus 13:3,8,9). It must have struck some of them as strange. There had been no more memorable moment in history since Noah and the flood. Why would they ever forget the strong hand of God and the way He had acted on their behalf?

But forget they did, and quickly at that. The book of Exodus tells us God took the people the long way to the promised land because He knew they weren't ready to see war. (Can we just run a thousand miles with the thought that God knows what we are ready to face and when?) He leads them through the wilderness toward the Red Sea in the visible form of a cloud by day and a pillar of fire by night. He never once took His eyes off them. But true to our own experience, their enemy pursued them. Pharaoh and his armies pressed in hard after having a change of mind. Who wants to do the physical work involved in building an empire?

> When Pharaoh drew near, the people of Israel lifted up their eyes, and behold, the Egyptians were marching after them, and they feared greatly. And the people of Israel cried out to the LORD. They said to Moses, "Is it because there are no graves in Egypt that you have taken us away to die in the wilderness? What have you done to us in bringing us out of Egypt? Is not this what we said to you in Egypt: 'Leave us alone that we may serve the Egyptians'? For it would have been better for us to serve the Egyptians than to die in the wilderness" (Exodus 14:10-12).

Drama. That's what we call incredible overstatements in our house. The problem was that the Israelites didn't know how their stories would end. But we do. The next morning Moses stretches out his hand and the Lord brings an east wind that blows the Red Sea back like a wall on each side. All night long, they must have huddled together knowing they were between the sea and a cloud of darkness that blocked Pharaoh's army. That was a scary night, with the enemy behind them and the storm blowing all around them. It wasn't in their foggiest imaginations that God could or would make that next move.

When they got to the other side, the celebration was deep and pure and joyous. Songs of worship flowed from their lips in praise to the God who delivered them. Just for kicks, you should take the time to read in Exodus 15 the song they sang on the banks after their rescue. The lines I find most telling are these: "The LORD is my strength and my song, and he has become my salvation" (verse 2) and "Who is like you, O LORD, among the gods? Who is like you, majestic in holiness, awesome in glorious deeds, doing wonders?" (verse 11).

It would seem to Caleb and to us that these people would remember the strong arm of God. When God told the spies to go into the promised land and survey it, as a chief from the tribe of Judah, Caleb was selected. What a privilege, what an honor to be among the first to see the land God had given them. And upon their return Caleb and his friend Joshua were full of faith. Interestingly, all 12 spies had seen the same land and spied the same giants and fortified cities. It's just that Caleb and Joshua recalled the deliverance from Egypt and remembered the promise of God.

Caleb says, "If the LORD delights in us, he will bring us into this land and give it to us, a land that flows with milk and honey. Only do not rebel against the LORD. And do not fear the people of the land, for they are bread for us. Their protection is removed from them, and the LORD is with us; do not fear them" (Numbers 14:8-9). And that's when his people picked up rocks to stone Caleb, Joshua, Moses, and Aaron.

The difference between being victorious in motherhood and gaining ground for the kingdom of God today is the same as it was for Caleb. It involves knowing our God and knowing His promises. The difference between desert and bounty in our faith all hinges on one thing: our ability to believe God.

A Real Enemy

It's time to have a frank conversation, because this motherhood thing is not a game. Scripture describes this life we're in as a war. "We do not wrestle against flesh and blood, but against the rulers, against the authorities, against the cosmic powers over this present darkness, against the spiritual forces of evil in the heavenly places" (Ephesians 6:12).

Part of me wants to shrug off and downplay this threat. I'm not one looking for the devil behind every bush, and I don't want you to be either. But God's Word is telling us that what we're wrestling against in our schools, in our governments, and yes, even in our homes has a dimension we may not be engaging in.

Jesus told us in John 10:10 that "the thief comes only to steal and kill and destroy. I came that they may have life and have it abundantly." Consider the agenda of the Enemy. He has come to steal from you and your children the peace Christ comes to offer, the joy in your family relationships, opportunities for legacies of faith, innocence from your children, and hope for change. He has come to kill. The Greek word for *kill* here can also mean "to butcher."[1] This isn't hypothetical killing. Satan comes to destroy us. Destroy our homes, our marriages, our churches, our testimonies. Steal, kill, destroy. Those are fighting words.

Peter warns us, "Be sober-minded; be watchful. Your adversary the devil prowls around like a roaring lion, seeking someone to devour" (1 Peter 5:8). These three passages are strong warnings from the heart of Christ, Paul, and Peter. This is business, ladies. We have an enemy. You have an enemy and his eyes are on your family. We have no cease-fire with the Enemy, no base to run to for a time-out or to take a breather. He is relentless, he is strong, and his agenda is clear. That should stop us cold in our tracks.

However, we also have good news. Our enemy, Satan, is a defeated foe. His time is short and he will not prevail. Greater still, if we are in Christ, we have the Holy Spirit taking up residence inside us and Christ is infinitely stronger than the Enemy.

> Little children, you are from God and have overcome them, for he who is in you is greater than he who is in the world (1 John 4:4).

This is a memory verse I often work on with my AWANA girls, and I've taught them to say it this way: "He who is in you [Jesus] is greater than he who is in the world [Satan]." He who is in you, friends, already defeated the Enemy when He rose from the grave, and His next event on the kingdom calendar is coming for us. At that time, the book of Revelation tells us, He will strike down His enemies with a word from His mouth.[2] This is not, nor has it ever been, a contest between two equals. There is absolutely no comparison in the strength of our God and the Enemy who threatens us.

> We must become warrior women.
> Brave kids need brave moms.

The problem, however, begins when we don't acknowledge that we are in the middle of a war, when we don't suit up for the battle we are engaged in, and when we don't walk in the victory appointed for us in reliance on Him. We must become warrior women. Brave kids need brave moms. We can't be moms who are wimps and raise children who walk bravely in the next generation.

One problem we have is addressed so perfectly by Beth Moore:

> The bride of Christ in our generation is nearly paralyzed by unbelief. Particularly in America! God is calling His bride to a fresh and lavish anointing of faith. He wants to put a fresh belief in our systems! We have been assigned to this world during vital days on the kingdom calendar. We have dropped our shield; therefore, we have never been more vulnerable to defeat. God is calling His church to draw the sword of the Spirit (the Word of God) and lift high the shield of faith.[3]

In his teaching about defense in the war against us, Paul tells believers, "In all circumstances take up the shield of faith, with which you can extinguish all the flaming darts of the evil one" (Ephesians 6:16). Our shield is our faith, which makes sense when we consider that faith in Christ is what allowed us to become members of the kingdom of God in the first place. Our belief that God loved us and wanted relationship with us was step one. We had to deep down be convinced that He was good and worth drawing close. We accepted that, when God told us through Scripture that we were sinful and lost, He was telling the truth. Further, we believed that, for reasons beyond our understanding, out of his unending love the Father sent Christ to die for us. We believed that He lives to be our Lord and wants us to follow Him and live in fellowship with Him.

So what is it about our faith that blocks the attack of the Enemy? If he can somehow convince us that God isn't who He says He is or we begin to question His heart toward us, unbelief sneaks in. This has always been the tactic. It began in the garden when Satan asked Eve, "Did God actually say?" (Genesis 3:1) and in between the lines the Enemy slid a small wedge between Eve and God. His effort would never have amounted to much; it would have been one fiery dart extinguished by the shield of Eve's faith. Except it wasn't. Because in her heart she began to question God's right to rule, as He had clearly established, and His heart toward her. Why shift to new tactics when the same ones work on us?

I'm beginning to realize it is faith that saves us, and continuing to believe that enables us to live victoriously and in strength on the path He has chosen for us. Scripture contains hundreds of references to believing God, but only a handful that discuss unbelief. I found that telling (and quicker to disseminate, if I'm being honest about it). Unbelief is a refusal to trust and it is poisonous in the life of a believer. It seems to be a condition we as mothers slide into rather than knowingly cannonball into.

The Abars

Did the Red Sea Generation believe their God? Did they believe He was who He said He was and that He would carry them safely to the place He called them? No, and they died because of unbelief and their steadfast refusal to trust God to do what He promised. The price was so high, and we would be absolutely fooling ourselves if we think unbelief inside us will cost us less. Unbelief drains power right out of mothers who want to pass faith to the next generation.

When Moses had died and the last of the Red Sea Generation was buried, God called to Joshua, Moses's servant. "Moses my servant is

dead. Now therefore arise, go over this Jordan, you and all this people, into the land that I am giving to them, to the people of Israel.
Every place that the sole of your foot will tread upon I have given to
you, just as I promised to Moses" (Joshua 1:2-3). The orders had not
changed; the leader had. The promise did not change; it remained the
same. The Israelites would have God's presence and power. To Joshua
God mentions a little something else:

> Be strong and courageous, for you shall cause this peo-
> ple to inherit the land that I swore to their fathers to give
> them. Only be strong and very courageous, being care-
> ful to do according to all the law that Moses my servant
> commanded you...that you may have good success wher-
> ever you go...Have I not commanded you? Be strong and
> courageous. Do not be frightened, and do not be dis-
> mayed, for the LORD your God is with you wherever you
> go (Joshua 1:6-7,9).

Joshua follows orders immediately and gives the people their three-
day warning. "Gather up your things; it's time to leave the wilderness."
The peoples' response is amazing and so full of faith.

> They answered Joshua, "All that you have commanded us
> we will do, and wherever you send us we will go. Just as we
> obeyed Moses in all things, so we will obey you. Only may
> the LORD your God be with you, as he was with Moses!
> Whoever rebels against your commandment and disobeys
> your words, whatever you command him, shall be put to
> death. Only be strong and courageous" (Joshua 1:16-18).

Dial in your attention on one simple observation. Three times
the Lord told Joshua to be strong and courageous, and when Joshua
turned to give orders to the people they heartily declared their commitment to obey. But don't miss that the Abars looked at their
leader and told him to be strong and courageous as well. Why?

Why would God and the people look at their leader and tell him to be courageous?

Because Joshua was afraid.

As mothers, the opportunities to be terrified, discouraged, and sometimes even mystified abound. The Abars would have had their heads in the wilderness sand not to acknowledge that giants were still in the land. They still had battles to face and enemies who wanted to destroy them, but this generation lifted up a shield of faith and put step over step into the land of promise.

Girls, time after time we will be called to actively believe God despite what our eyes can see and our minds can understand. I can promise that as the Abars walked into the first battle in the new land, nobody could have predicted the way God would lead them into victory. Jericho was a fortified city with high walls and mighty men of valor inside (Joshua 6:2). The battle plan would involve taking a quiet walk around the walled city for six days, and on the seventh day a great big hike and then trumpets and shouting. When the walls fell, don't you know that the children of Israel turned to each other and said, "Well, I'll be. I never saw that coming."

As mamas, we will face opportunity after opportunity to stand before a wall and trust God to move it. Ephesians 1:19 tells us "incomparably great power" exists for those of us who believe (NIV). The power God used when He raised Christ from the dead is now ready to be unleashed in the lives of those who are willing to take Him at His word. And to do that, we must become certain of the promises He has made to us. We must know His character and be students of His ways. We can't actively believe a God we do not know. Psalm 9:10 promises, "Those who know your name put their trust in you, for you, O LORD, have not forsaken those who seek you." There is nothing passive about faith walking.

Apply Faith

The choice to believe God in an active way presents itself to us every morning. Before our feet hit the floor, we have the choice in front of us to either thank God that He is directing the day and commit ourselves to Him or to allow the pressures of the day and the hazards of motherhood to direct our thoughts. If I believe God is present in my day, then I will act accordingly and my children will catch on quickly.

> Modeling faith begins with our children catching us believing God.

For me this means thanking God for His presence in our home, thanking Him for His provision, spending time reflecting on what He is doing and pointing it out to my children. Rarely do I have to conjure up ways to believe God in front of my family. Every day stories in the news raise a fear flag in my mind, and these are no different from battles faced on the far side of the Jordan River. My children have to hear me say, "Yes, the world is scary right now, but God promises us His presence." "There may be poor leadership in our government right now, but we have a God who tells us He is the one who sets up and removes authorities and we can trust Him." Or "This is difficult right now but we will see God be faithful to us." Because here's the thing, modeling faith begins with our children catching *us* believing God. Children must be taught that God is faithful, that He will provide, that He is enough, that He fights for us, and that we can trust Him.

But How, Lord?

When the calling of God seems impossible to fulfill because of the lack of resources in our hands, it's time to watch for a miracle. Time and again, our family has had the opportunity to watch God catch those who step out to follow His leading. My guess is you have seen that too.

Several years back our close friends and pastor, Ryan and Stacy, felt called to pursue their second adoption. Stacy is the most petite, adorable, crafty, resourceful friend, whose home looks like it could be in *Better Homes and Gardens*. She is also one of the most frugal people I've ever met. They've had to be frugal as they have lived on a modest, small-town pastor's salary with their four blond boys, and at that point with one adopted daughter. When we first began talking about the stirring in their hearts to adopt again, we knew their resources were minuscule; they had been totally financially depleted by their last adoption. But they were reading books about the orphan crisis in the world, and when Stacy began looking at waiting children more heavily, we knew God was up to something.

That's when the conversations became more intense. The financial need was great, but even greater, the more they learned about the orphan crisis, the more their hearts broke for HIV positive orphans. The first time Stacy and I talked about the idea of their adopting an HIV positive child was on the way to a conference with our husbands riding in the front and us huddled in the back. We talked about what she was learning about the care of HIV positive children and their life expectancy, about the risk to their own family (minimal), and then about the financial resources needed to bring another little one home. As we prayed with them and began to apply faith with them, we believed God would bring another child home despite the money necessary, and we believed He would help them learn to keep all their family protected from any disease He called them to bring into their home.

The next 12 months were filled with joy and expectation as we watched God provide on every level. He brought them a new vehicle that would seat their family of eight, they received grants from adoption organizations like Show Hope, and we saw the body of Christ pull off the craziest garage sale that raised thousands. One man paid $200 for a lampshade. Our kids manned a lemonade stand in the front yard that said, "Bring our friend home" and had a picture of little Lucy. All of us wept at the end of the day as we watched the Lord provide for the plan He dreamed up. When Ryan and Stacy and Lucy arrived back in the United States, tears poured from all of our eyes and we gave glory to God. Where God leads, God provides. You'd better believe we stood in that airport and held that baby girl and then told our kids the story of how God did this breathtaking thing.

The Abars applied faith and fought many battles, but they left the job of torch passing incomplete. Scripture tells us the people of Israel fought battles together to drive out the enemy, and then Joshua dismissed the people to go take possession of the land:

> The people served the LORD all the days of Joshua, and all
> the days of the elders who outlived Joshua, who had seen
> all the great work that the LORD had done for Israel...And
> all that generation also were gathered to their fathers. And
> there arose another generation after them who did not
> know the LORD or the work that he had done for Israel
> (Judges 2:7,10).

Isn't that a terrible letdown? The Abars, after all they had been through with the Lord, after walking hand in hand through victory they could not explain through any human means, raised an unbelieving generation. Of course, I don't know what happened. But I wonder if somewhere along the way they stopped talking to their kids about the wonders of God they had seen along the way. Did they stop orally rehearsing the way God provided for them in the desert and protected them in the battles when they arrived at a place of safety? If so, we would be wise to take note of any situation that causes us to settle back and not actively live our faith. I once heard John Piper say if we aren't discussing Christ with our kids on a regular basis, we are teaching them—whether or not we mean to—that Christ isn't relevant.[4]

Christ is always relevant, my friends. Always present. Always pertinent. Always invested.

Our job as parents is to actively apply faith over all matters. We are the ones who bear the responsibility of believing that this life really is all about Jesus. As Romans 11:36 puts it, "From him and through him and to him are all things." Christ is always relevant, my friends. Always present. Always pertinent. Always invested. We simply are invited to apply faith.

But what if we can't find the way to apply faith? What if we are just trying to put one foot in front of the other and the fog or the grief or the fear sucks the life and hope and faith right out of us?

Help My Unbelief

The man was surely at the end of his rope. His son, his only child, had been disturbed for years. Hopelessness and fear must have been his constant companion as he watched the life of his child being stolen away. Where I'm from we don't often attribute suffering and sickness to demon possession, but in this instance, the father is convinced that's what's wrong. The Bible gives three accounts of this scene, each adding detail to the others, but all in harmony and agreement about what occurred. The lesson found in the middle is for us moms trying to live out this faith thing.

The Gospels tell us Jesus had been up the mountain praying with his inner-circle of three—Peter, James, and John. Suddenly Jesus is changed before their eyes. He is gleaming with glory and His clothing is blindingly white. Moses and Elijah show up and spend time talking with Jesus about the last leg of His ministry and fulfilling His purpose on earth. Meanwhile, the disciples are filled with fear—the good kind. They are amazed and in awe of the transfigured Jesus, who is now sporting some of the glory that He has had since the beginning of the world, and they are nearly overcome.

Peter begins talking because he doesn't know what to say. Read it. The Scripture actually says that! Not that I have ever started speaking because I didn't know what to say...The rebuke this time comes not from Jesus, but from His heavenly Father. "This is my Son, whom I love...Listen to him!" (Matthew 17:5 NIV). Can you imagine hearing that rebuke from God Himself? I just can't even. One commentary I read says their fear grew until the final moments when Jesus touched them and told them to "rise, and have no fear" (Matthew 17:7).[5] When they pulled their faces off the ground, Jesus was alone again and He charged them to tell no one what they had just seen. What had they witnessed on that mountain? They saw Jesus robed in the glory that has been His for all of time.

As the three and Jesus headed back down to Caesarea Philippi, at some distance they saw a crowd and heard arguing. The crowd quickly ran to greet them, excited and amazed that Jesus was with them. I imagine the three were dying to tell the others what had just happened. But the squabbling in the center of the crowd drew the question, "What are you arguing with them about?" That's when this tired, broken father stepped forward.

> Teacher, I brought my son to you, for he has a spirit
> that makes him mute. And whenever it seizes him, it
> throws him down, and he foams and grinds his teeth
> and becomes rigid...from childhood. And it has often
> cast him into fire and into water, to destroy him. But if
> you can do anything, have compassion on us and help us
> (Mark 9:17-18, 21-22).

Hear the pain in his voice. "I brought You my son. Do you see these burn marks on him? That's where he's thrown himself into the fire. He looks like an epileptic when he's thrown to the ground. I hate watching him suffer. Please. Have mercy on my son. Have compassion on us. Please, help us." We can feel his pain in some way if we try. He can't let his boy out of his sight because he's trying to be killed by something living inside him. If he turns his back, his son falls into a fire or into water. The demon inside his boy is ruthless and has stolen both of their lives. Jesus asks him, "How long has this been happening to him?" and the father sighs. "From child-hood" (Mark 9:21). That's such a long time to pray and hope for a miracle, and he is so weary and worn-out from hoping and fighting and wrestling. Now he's brought his boy to this place and the con-vulsions begin again. "If you can do anything, have compassion on *us*, and help *us*" (emphasis added). It isn't just his son who has the problem; it's both of them.

Jesus must have looked the man squarely in the eye. "'If you can'! All things are possible for one who believes" (Mark 9:23). On the heels of the transfiguration, three disciples are in the crowd that just watched Jesus miraculously transform an average situation into an encounter with the living God, but this father was not one of them. He was just in the middle of a situation that hurt, knowing his resources were too few and his time was almost up. He was tired and worn.

Have you been there? Has it taken so long for God to walk into a situation where you needed Him that it looked almost impossible, only to have someone play the "believe" card?

> Immediately the father of the child cried out and said, "I believe; help my unbelief!" (Mark 9:24).

That is the moment the healing began for both father and son. After commanding the demon to leave, Jesus took the boy by the hand and raised him to his feet. Don't be fooled into thinking he was the only one healed in that moment. The father's unbelief was healed in that moment also. Unbelief is a forfeiture of power that belongs to us, and there is incomparably great power available to those who know and believe their God. When unbelief comes, and it will, we must own it and ask for more faith.

Hebrews 3:19 tells us the Red Sea Generation was unable to enter the promised land because of unbelief. Let's steadfastly refuse to allow the Enemy to lie to us and to let unbelief blind us to the promise of God waiting for us just around the corner.

Father,

How can it be that unbelief has sneaked into the corners of my life when You are so tremendously worthy of being believed? Forgive me for rehearsing the pain, the tension, and the fear instead of Your promises. I want to be found believing You—not just believing in You, but believing that You are working right now in my situation. Allow my children to see and hear me speaking of Your faithfulness. As far as it depends on me, I want the next generation to know You and the works You have done for the children of Israel and for us as a family. You are a good Father and I believe You. Amen.

7

Reflect

To acquire knowledge, one must study; but to
acquire wisdom, one must observe.
—MARILYN VOS SAVANT

My friend Staci is a boss. Not only does she have four great kids she's raising to be heroes of the faith, but she is also ridiculously athletic. She is the varsity basketball coach for our high school team, and it is not unusual for Staci's cheering section to be as loud as the student section. Our community loves her. We live in the sticks where high speed internet continues to be a foreign wish, so it is not unusual for us to run into each other at the library.

Within a day or two of a game, Staci sits in the library, hat pulled down low, earphones on, watching replay footage of her last game. She's in the zone there too. One day I pulled up a seat next to her and asked her about it because we'd been at the game the night before. She slid over a little and explained. Staci sits and watches her players, looking for anything she missed when the ball was live. With the crowd cheering, the refs running back and forth, and plays running, it's easy to miss things. Staci strengthens her team by watching the game again, looking for what her girls did well and reviewing what they did poorly.

That is exactly what parenthood requires. Time, space, and a heart prepared for some reflection.

Take care, and keep your soul diligently (Deuteronomy 4:9).

It's blessed hard to keep anything diligently these days. A few minutes ago my phone rang with an automated message reminding me of an open house at my children's school tomorrow night. It also triggered a ring on my husband's phone and auto texted both of us. That's four messages for one event, multifaceted because we'll have two children who need to find their lockers, meet teachers, and plan the quickest routes to the important things, like the car pickup line and the cafeteria. Our other two children are still elementary students who don't need to be present, and let's be honest, who wants their whole family trekking to 12 different classrooms anyway? This open house will require us to find childcare for at least a portion of it. The message also said there will be a parent meeting for students who wish to play sports next year. We will have one child who fits that category, so we will now be considering driving separately to the event. In summary, one event, four messages, one babysitter, two vehicles, six spinning plates.

This stage of life—the one I have affectionately begun to call organized chaos, or taxi cab for short—makes tending anything seem like a far-fetched idea. You may not have four children and a farmer for a husband. You may be a single mom with a crazy-hard life, just trying to breathe. You may have 12 children like some of our favorite people in the world, or you may have only one. Regardless, even one child makes you busy. Busy, busy, busy.

I wish you could come over right now and pull up a rocking chair on my front porch. We'd talk about the four acres of grass that surround our home we mow and how I wish I had time to weed the flower bed in the front. If you were here and you looked closely, you would see the pine trees we planted in the front when we built the house seven years ago.

Mike called and told me he was buying 50 trees from the conservation district to plant in our new yard. It had been a cornfield for decades before that, nary a tree to be seen, yet I figured 50 seemed excessive. But I know to always trust my farmer when it comes to growing things. When the order came in and he told me he was going to pick up the trees, I wondered if we would be taking a trailer along. He said, "No, I'll just grab them in my pickup truck." Well, immediately I began adjusting my expectation to trees smaller than I'd originally envisioned. When he pulled into the driveway, I walked out, baby on hip, to assess the situation. Mike set a bucket down on the driveway and we both started laughing. There, tied into a tight little bundle you could grab with two hands, were 50 baby trees. No wonder they were a bargain.

During the first year, it was all we could do to grow our three kids, the four acres of grass, and plant and water the 50 trees. During Mike's busy season, I would mow the lawn when the kids were napping, but it was not unusual for the thin grass to grow six to eight inches tall between mows. It's tough to keep a yard and a family. So one night, in my haste to lessen the embarrassment over my tall lawn, I mowed over 20 of the baby trees. The grass had just creeped up, and by the time I realized it I'd taken out 40 percent of our landscaping. The following year we weeded around the trees, watered them, saved them from drought—and ran over another 20 percent. It really is a miracle we have any trees at all.

I have this theory that you can have great kids or a great lawn, but not both, at least not at our home. For us it has become a matter of priorities during the season of life we're in. Every year our yard has looked a little different as what has needed attention has changed. Some years we have had a beautiful garden; other years, like the summer I was pregnant with our fourth, I couldn't stand the smell of the tomato plants, I was sick as a dog, and the plants were out of control. We had a pumpkin growing on top of our tomato cage.

Keeping things diligently takes time and focus. It requires a determined spirit and a close eye ready to weed out what might pollute or overtake whatever is being grown. The same is true for souls, both ours and our children's. Moses told the children of Israel to tend their souls with diligence "lest you forget the things that your eyes have seen, and lest they depart from your heart all the days of your life" (Deuteronomy 4:9). That means they were to lean over and examine their lives, looking for anything that didn't align with the law the Lord had given them.

That truth applies to us as well. We must spend time asking the Holy Spirit to help us reflect on the condition of our souls, our lives, and our families. In the hustle and bustle of normal family life, it's easy to overlook what must be uprooted and pulled out before it topples the tomato cage or gets run over by the lawn mower of life. Mark my words, too, that there is always room for more tending. Romans 8:29 tells us God is in the business of making us look like Jesus, conforming us into the image of His Son. And short of heaven, there is always room for improvement. We'd be wise to give our hearts a long look while we tend to the matter of teaching and shaping our children.

I can think of two men in Scripture who may have personally been trying to live lives that honored the Lord, but who radically failed to tend to their children. The results were devastating.

Epic Fail

Eli and his sons were priests before the Lord in a town called Shiloh. Theirs was a job they were born into, not one they aspired to. But please don't let them off the hook in your mind. By definition, priests stood as intermediaries between God and man and they had the occupational responsibility of making sacrifices on behalf of the people to atone for their sins. The Lord went to great lengths to regulate those who could serve Him in that capacity, and He went further still in explaining exactly how important the atoning of sin would be before Him. If we fast-forward the tape to the New Testament, we learn that the sacrificial system would always fail. Every sin committed by people has a corresponding consequence, and there would never be enough animal blood to cover the sin of man. The blood of

God's perfect Son was required to finally pay that debt once and for all (1 Peter 3:18).

Serving as priest before the Lord in the Old Testament meant business. They gave offerings for their own sins and offerings for the endless stream of people who came to them. They made peace offerings, sin offerings, wave offering, festival offerings, yearly offerings...and the list went on and on. One can easily imagine the ramifications of what they were doing could easily lose their potency after year upon year. It's not too big a stretch to imagine that Eli's sons, Hophni and Phinehas, had lost the wonder of sins atoned—if they had ever found the wonder of it all in the first place.

> The sons of Eli were worthless men. They did not know
> the LORD (1 Samuel 2:12).

These are harsh words from the Holy Spirit, right? *Worthless.* What on God's green earth could make the One who created those boys call them worthless? It's telling to start with what we know, and right at the top we know they were attending services regularly at the tabernacle. Scratch that; they were the ones conducting the services. Yet "they did not know the LORD" (1 Samuel 2:12). The account goes on to describe the wickedness and perversion that came during Eli's sons' corrupted service. They viewed the sacrificial duty as something that could be mocked, and they had become irreverent in their services. They took meat that belonged to the Lord, the cuts of their choosing, and if necessary used force with those making the offering. They had become a bully squad with a hankering for marbled steaks. "The sin of the young men was very great in the sight of the LORD, for the men treated the offering of the LORD with contempt" (1 Samuel 2:17). Eli's sons were notorious in Israel for immorality and corruption.

> Eli was very old, and he kept hearing all that his sons were
> doing to all Israel, and how they lay with the women who
> were serving at the entrance to the tent of meeting. And

he said to them, "Why do you do such things? For I hear
of your evil dealings from all these people. No, my sons;
it is no good report that I hear the people of the LORD
spreading abroad. If someone sins against a man, God will
mediate for him, but if someone sins against the LORD,
who can intercede for him?" But they would not listen to
the voice of their father, for it was the will of the LORD to
put them to death (1 Samuel 2:22-25).

As a parent, it is terrifying for me to report the truth of what God
says about Hophni and Phinehas's sin. If we were friends with Eli's
wife, we might have been upset privately about the corruption we
saw building in her sons, their brazen disregard for the Lord, and the
girls they were running around with. If we were truly good and caring friends, we might have even gone to Eli and his wife, as some people obviously had, with all the information and tried to point out our
concerns. Most of us, however, would not hold Eli's sons' behavior
against him. It would make us vulnerable to people holding our children's misdeeds against us. But this is precisely what the Lord does.

God said to Eli, "Why then do you scorn my sacrifices and my
offerings that I commanded for my dwelling, and honor your sons
above me?" (1 Samuel 2:29).

It may be easy for us to easily brush aside the sins of our children
as not as devious and brazen as those of Hophni and Phinehas, but
all their sins separate our children from God's plan for them. All of
them. Do you believe that? While we might believe they will outgrow
"lesser" behaviors like selfishness, lying, and whining, are we willing
to gamble the future of our children with our passivity? Will we skirt
addressing and tending to the business of their hearts because we are
tired, worn down, or distracted? The thought sobers me. What Eli's
sons needed most was a father who honored God above his own sons.
When God considered the lack of discipline Eli showed his sons, He
chose to call the matter one of honor.

Scripture commands us time and again to "fear the Lord and serve

Him only," and I wonder if at the core of Eli was a fear of man greater than the fear of God. Did Eli fear his sons would turn against him, or withhold their love? Did he fear that firing them and removing them from the priesthood would prevent them from finding other careers, or that they would be shunned? Regardless, by the time Eli addressed the problem of the irreverence and sin in his children, they were swimming in the burning anger of God and their hearts were hard. Later the Lord told Samuel He would not only be punishing the sin of his sons, but also the parental failure. "I declare to [Eli] that I am about to punish his house forever, for the iniquity that he knew, because his sons were blaspheming God, and he did not restrain them" (1 Samuel 3:13).

Lean in for a minute, friend, and listen deep. Our job as parents is to image God to our children. While society is modeling passivity, and even child centeredness, we will be doing a grievous disservice to our children if we don't gently tend their hearts. At the root of the word *discipline* is the word *disciple*, and that is no accident. Our goal in raising our heroes has at the heart of it disciple making. Discipline by definition is not merely doling out consequences, though surely that is a part of it, but it also looks forward and actively teaches, instructs, and prepares our kids for the path ahead of them. While this must be measured in love, gently (never abusively) and diligently, the pressures of society to allow our children to be "free range" disciples is unbiblical. Our heavenly Father proves His love to us by His discipline. Consider the following:

> The LORD corrects those he loves, just as a father corrects a
> child in whom he delights (Proverbs 3:12 NLT).

> The LORD disciplines those he loves, and he punishes each
> one he accepts as his child (Hebrews 12:6 NLT).

Jesus Himself says, "Those whom I love I rebuke and discipline. So be earnest and repent" (Revelation 3:19 NIV).

The discipline of the Lord proves His love and acceptance of us as His children. It makes us His legitimate children, in whom He is investing His time and attention. In turn, our response as BRAVE moms must be to view the work of reflecting on the condition of our children's hearts and doing the work necessary to tend them as a part of our love for them. Proverbs 13:24 (NIV) says, "Whoever spares the rod hates their children, but the one who loves their children is careful to discipline them." Don't be so turned off by the "rod" portion of this text that you miss the idea that if we love our children we will diligently discipline them.

This may mean:

- We leave a cart full of groceries to address a temper tantrum in a grocery store.
- We issue consequences that may be inconvenient for us, like taking away electronic devices or their hour of television time.
- We address the heart issue behind the complaining and teach them about the sin of discontentment and ingratitude.
- We don't accept sibling spats as normal between brothers and sisters and instead encourage them to serve one another in love.
- We have them sit out an activity for the good of the whole family rather than allow them to continue to be involved at the cost of relationships, money, and time together.
- We require first-time, immediate obedience with a good attitude. If they don't obey the first time we instruct them, it isn't immediate, or it isn't with a good attitude, it isn't obedience because immediate obedience is the Father's expectation of us.

Practicing consistent discipline is often much harder on me than it is on my children. These are the choices we make every day to engage with our kids, and they are neither convenient nor fun, but they are right. So we get up and do the hard work of training our kids, because that's our job.

The second epic failure in parenting is brought to us by none other than the king whom Scripture calls the man after God's heart (Acts 13:22). David did many things well, but unfortunately, diligently tending his children's hearts was not one of them.

David's oldest child, Amnon, is impressionable, has chosen terrible friends, and plans and executes the rape of his half-sister, Tamar. During the course of the rape, Tamar begs her brother to stop and explains that if Amnon would only ask their father, David would give her to him in marriage, which was forbidden by God's law.

Whether or not David would have broken that law, he learned of his daughter's rape from his son and did nothing. Nothing. You read that right. "When King David heard of all these things, he was very angry" (2 Samuel 13:21). If you read this passage in your Bible, it might have a footnote that reads something like this: the "Dead Sea Scroll, Septuagint add But he would not punish his son Amnon, because he loved him, since he was his firstborn."[1] The reason we don't find that in our current manuscript is because scholars aren't absolutely certain it was in the original text. But both of those quoted, the Dead Sea Scrolls and the Septuagint, are reliable manuscripts.

Regardless, how could he and why would he let this sin go unaddressed and unpunished? The parental failure and passivity begin to mount. We see no mention of David attending to and ministering to Tamar. We cannot overlook that an integral part of tending our children's hearts is ministering to them and meeting with them in love in their biggest hurts, shame, and pain. This oversight was not missed by another of David's sons, Absalom, who immediately took in the broken Tamar and began to plot his half-brother Amnon's death. David ignored the icy tension between the brothers, as Scripture tells us that Absalom refused to speak to his brother.

When Absalom has Amnon assassinated, he flees, and David's

heart is torn in two. "The spirit of the king longed to go out to Absalom, because he was comforted about Amnon, since he was dead"
(2 Samuel 13:39). Talk about *Days of Our Lives*, and this soap opera
isn't half over. Absalom goes on to try to take the crown from his father
by force (2 Samuel 15).

My guess is that David and Eli both dearly loved their children.
Perhaps to such a depth that they fell into a trap of believing that telling their children no would hurt them. The minute we put our children's comfort or happiness in front of their obedience to the Lord, we
have believed a lie. The Enemy would have us believe God's ways are
restrictive, or the job of disciplining our children is too much for us.
The truth is God's ways may not bring immediate happiness, but they
bring lasting joy, peace, and a life that honors the Lord. Further, sin
never stays small and confined. It may begin that way, but left unaddressed it will burn our families like a wildfire. In both cases, what
probably started as a small character flaw left unchecked became a
huge issue that brought death (literally) in both families.

Even the most godly parents can't ultimately control all their
children's behavior and choices, especially as they grow into adults.
However, let's always be faithful to prayerfully, wisely, and diligently
encourage our children to walk in the ways of the Lord. King David's
family was marred by tragedy, but he did finish well. His last words
to his son Solomon were an example to all of us.

> I am about to go the way of all the earth. Be strong, and
> show yourself a man, and keep the charge of the Lord
> your God, walking in his ways and keeping his statutes,
> his commandments, his rules, and his testimonies, as it
> is written in the Law of Moses, that you may prosper in
> all that you do and wherever you turn, that the Lord
> may establish his word that he spoke concerning me, say-
> ing, "If your sons pay close attention to their way, to walk
> before me in faithfulness with all their heart and with all

their soul, you shall not lack a man on the throne of Israel"
(1 Kings 2:2-4).

Praying They Are Caught

One of our dearest friends, Ben, has parents worth their weight in
gold. They diligently tended their son's heart as he was growing, and
the result has been the best friend my husband has ever known. Ben
is a godly, humble servant of the Lord, who is also one of the most
gifted Bible teachers I have ever met. Ben is fun and quick to encourage others, which is such a fun example for us. But every once in a
while a gleam in his eyes hints that at some point in his life he may
have been mischief itself.

Ben tells us his parents planted Scripture in his heart, and they
often reminded him that they prayed he would be caught in his sin.
When we first heard that, both Mike and I laughed heartily, imagin-
ing a young Ben caught in a prank. He let us know, however, that he
was grateful for those prayers and for the ways the Lord has answered
them. He told us unequivocally that the Lord had granted his parents' request and that he always gets caught in wrongdoing. This has
become one of my favorite requests of the Lord, though it isn't without risk. Several things may even keep parents from praying along
these lines, beginning with:

Fear—What will I find if I search their closet or read their text
history? What happens if I pull on the thread of my child's sin and
the whole thing comes unraveled? Or perhaps even, what if my child
pulls away from me emotionally, spiritually, or, heaven forbid, even
physically?

Embarrassment—What will people think of my child, or even
me, if this behavior is exposed?

Shame—What does this say about my parenting? What would
our church friends think if they knew my child did this? Does this
mean I'm failing as a mother?

Discomfort—Why would I choose to upset our lives? It's easier to live in ignorance than to open the door to the unknowns or deal with the discipline this will require, right?

Mirror—Admitting that they are doing this wrong will also shine a light on my own sins. How can I address issues in them, like lying, disrespect of authority, or immorality when I have modeled this behavior?

These are all real issues, real risks. However, without a doubt the rewards for praying for early sin detection and that our kids would be caught in their sin is infinitely more valuable than anything it costs us. I've thought a lot about what would inspire a parent to pray like this (I've even consulted Ben) and I think it has less to do with what we risk than with what we believe. We pray "Help us catch them" because we believe that:

- All sin separates my children from God and that separation hurts them (Isaiah 59:1-2; 1 John 1:6-9).
- Purity and holiness is God's will for our children and that we are praying for His will for them to be accomplished in them (1 Peter 1:15-16; 2 Peter 3:11,14).
- Being caught will provide us the opportunity to teach them right from wrong and model grace, mercy, reconciliation, and forgiveness. And all those things look like Jesus (2 Corinthians 5:18-21; Ephesians 4:32).
- Learning the consequences of being caught will discourage them from hiding sin down the road (2 Corinthians 7:9-11).
- Caring enough to teach them about authority and boundaries now will protect them from developing a spirit of rebellion (Romans 13:1-5).
- "Getting away with it" only builds a callus in their hearts toward sins and the lies and shame only become deeper and more painful when that callus is ripped off (Ecclesiastes 12:14; 2 Corinthians 7:10).

I would much rather pull out the tender root of a weed now than a full-sized oak tree rooted down deep in the future.

So what do we pray? Something like this:

> *Father, I want to train _____ to love and obey You. I'm asking You to make me aware when _____ is making choices that don't honor You. If they are breaking Your law, or developing heart attitudes that need addressing, I pray You will bring these things to light. I believe You discipline those You love. Please prompt me to ask good questions, or to sense Your Spirit's nudge when I need to dig deeper. I'm asking that _____ would be caught in their sin, and that I would react as You would, in step with Your Spirit, loving mercy and forgiveness.*

That's a BRAVE prayer, friends. It was an equal parts horror and honor to have the Lord answer this prayer when I caught one of our children trying to steal a small trinket in a store. We hadn't even left the store when the Spirit prompted me to check on my little sweetie. With cheeks flushed and sorrowful eyes, my child revealed the small toy stuffed in a pocket. It was an embarrassing moment for both of us, one etched in both of our minds. But we have each thanked the Lord that we could address the issue at six years old rather than later. The smaller the weed, the easier the pulling.

It isn't enough to address only our children's failures. Great parents need to know their children's strengths as well. If we are the ones guiding them to the path they should take (Proverbs 22:6), shouldn't we know well the people whom we are guiding? This depth of knowledge requires observation and study, a commitment well worth the effort.

Smitten

When Mike and I were dating, I studied that man. He was so different from any guy I had known or dated in the past. He loved the Lord, was disciplined, and led our relationship from day one by implementing boundaries. He was a farm boy who valued hard work, his family, and the land. He was steady and frugal, slow to anger, and even in the beginning I could tell he was discerning. His family tree had wide branches. After learning more about them, I would add to a family tree, including aunts, uncles, cousins, and grandparents. I found him fascinating, and as I learned, my heart toward him grew. I understood his passions, his giftings, and in what he found humor. Simultaneously, he let me in on his need for growth in areas where he felt insecure and on what concerned him.

All these tiny details seemed like vital pieces of information to digest and implement into our relationship. I was praying for Mike and asking how I could support him and honor him.

As I've rehearsed those first tender memories with my farmer, I've become convinced that I did something right during that time. I became a student of my future husband, gathering important details, considering them, and implementing a strategy based on what I learned. As time has passed, I've learned to gather the same information about the children God has given us. Honestly, I ask the same 20 or so questions of my friends, family, and sometimes even strangers (see Reflection Questions, page 243). Then I lean forward and try to listen close. My motto about everything is "On Paper on Purpose." More often than not, I have a working chart of the answers about my friends and family, and because people change, the answers on my loved ones' charts are never stagnant. However, simply asking questions and recording answers will never lead to a well-tended heart.

The *R* in the acronym BRAVE is for reflection because we must take what we observe and learn and turn them into prayers. My own effort to identify all the needs of my child's heart will turn up lacking, but our God will never fail. If we ask Him to reveal truth we need to see in our children, He will certainly be faithful to answer. These responses in turn become prayers for wisdom, insight, help, provision, thanksgiving, and protection for each aspect of our family's life. Reflection is the antithesis of distracted and indifferent; it leans forward and takes notes.

Reflecting well requires great balance and wisdom, and both will be given to us as we ask the Lord. As we prayerfully reflect on the condition of our children's hearts, we must train our eyes to include what is not going well. Reflection cannot lead to nagging and a critical spirit, but must instead offer loving and kind words in season. Mothers must be the first to spot wins, spiritual fruit, discernment, love, patience, giftings, and strengths in their children and bring them into the light in a loving and encouraging way.

Practically, I take my charts and mental notes and find Scriptures that speak to the needs and flaws I see in my children.

- Are they complainers? I pray they will "do everything without grumbling or arguing" (Philippians 2:14 NIV) and in turn be filled with gratitude.
- Are they making poor choices in the friends they choose? I pray they will walk with the wise and become wise (Proverbs 13:20).
- Are they fearful? I thank God that He gave them "a spirit not of fear but of power and love and self-control" (2 Timothy 1:7).

The list goes on and on. I'm trying to identify the root of the negative behavior or attitude I see being manifested—lying, disobedience, pride, selfishness, greed, and envy. Most recently, I've been praying that God will develop in two of my kids' tongues that which will overflow with the law of kindness (Proverbs 31:26).

Sometimes as the Lord brings sin patterns to light, Mike and I ultimately see changes we need to make in our parenting strategy. It is our desire to spur on the godliness we see and diligently shore up any weaknesses we find. When my friend Staci reviews the basketball game tapes, it is not enough for her to see the problems; the retraining, reteaching, and practice that happens next allows her team to be victorious. We all need that strategy in parenting.

This all requires time and energy, but I find the process of reflection deeply rewarding. Everyone wants a friend who is paying attention to them and their needs. Everyone. One totally unforeseen by-product, however, has been the reflection that has occurred in me. The Holy Spirit always seems to tend my heart as I identify and tend the hearts of my children. I must stay humble before the Lord as there is always room for improvement, and often occasions for my own repentance. I like what I see happening within our family and friends. It seems, after all, that everyone values being known.

> Lord,
> How we value being known by You. I find such comfort in knowing You are intimately acquainted with all my thoughts and ways. You know my giftings, my strengths, and my weaknesses. I need You to help me identify these same things in my children. I want to know them well so I can disciple them well. Help me to be observant, seeing what merits praise and encouragement and to catch them when they've strayed from Your best so I can lovingly point them back to Your truth. I want to be a student of these masterpieces You've given me. You give good gifts, Lord. Thank You. Amen.

8

Ask Forgiveness

God doesn't seek for golden vessels, and does not
ask for silver ones, but He must have clean ones.
—Dwight L. Moody

I'm that mom—the one who wants the perfect first day of school for her children. The one who gets up at the crack of dawn to ensure that even if we don't have another perfect morning in the whole school year, we will have a perfect morning on day one. This is complete with hot breakfasts, clean and maybe new outfits, and always first-day-of-school signs and pictures.

The only problem is at least one of my kids is always extremely nervous for the day ahead and a little edgy. Every year. When my expectations aren't met and all our emotions are running high, it is easy for me to lose my cool. And this isn't even slightly hypothetical.

"Smile. A real smile. Stand up straight. Look at me. No, put your backpack down and fix your shirt. How did you already get toothpaste on your shirt? Hold your sign straight! Why can't you smile? You are wrecking the picture. Why does this have to happen every year?"

This year I got pictures of everyone holding their signs, but I expressed my disappointment and frustration in words and I'm sure body language. It got ugly. I was leaving for a Moms in Prayer staff meeting in California at noon, and I needed to be packed and ready to go. I was trying to be very present in the morning with the kids, knowing I would be missing the face-to-face debriefing time when they got home that afternoon. I was just trying so hard to make a moment we would all remember.

Oh, we'll remember it all right, but it will go down as the year Mom raised her voice at the kid who couldn't (wouldn't?) smile. Then my oldest jumped in and told me to give her a break, that she was just nervous. Instead of listening, I turned to him, embarrassed, and yelled, "I will be the mom here, okay?" Which just hurt him. At that point, my husband drove into the driveway, and instead of letting him hug and encourage everyone, I let him have it about how uncooperative everyone was being. It wasn't until we were all piled into the van that I stopped fussing long enough to hear sniffling and the quiet voice of the Holy Spirit: *Lee, the things on your agenda this morning were temporary. What about the stuff that is eternal?*

In the quiet of the car, I began to pray.

Lord, please forgive me. I have run over my family this morning. I have been selfish in my motives and expectations. I have responded in anger and been slow to look from the kids' perspectives. I have been harsh and aggressive instead of loving and gentle. I need Your forgiveness. I have sinned against You and the kids, and I am so sorry.

Then I turned to my kids and told them, "Honeys, Mama has had a rotten attitude this morning. I wanted everything to look perfect instead of focusing on what was most important—what was going on inside you. I raised my voice and spoke unkindly and was inconsiderate. I need your forgiveness, and I'd like to start again. Will you guys forgive me?"

They always do.

> I wasn't very far into motherhood when I began to realize that some of the misbehavior and attitude problems in my kids were caused in part by the actions and attitudes of their mother.

Perfect parents do not exist. Occasionally, I feel like telling the kids that the quarters I find in our laundry machines will be used to fund their counseling as adults. I can wake up to a peaceful house, make a cup of coffee, spend an hour with the Lord, and even pray for the day that lies ahead of us all...and then walk five feet into my "not a morning person" daughter's room and need to hit my knees in repentance again.

I wasn't very far into motherhood when I began to realize that some of the misbehavior and attitude problems in my kids were caused in part by the actions and attitudes of their mother. While each of them proved at a young age that they were wicked in their own right, I can't deny that sometimes their meltdowns were age-related behavior when I had overcommitted us and stretched them thin. I've snapped when I felt as though they were being disrespectful or taking advantage of me. I've been known to be selfish when they've interrupted my sleep, to raise my voice when it wasn't necessary or helpful, and to fail to listen when I hurt their feelings. The truth is just so obvious to me. I'm not perfect, and I'm pretty sure you aren't either.

Cultivating an Atmosphere of Grace

Our job as mothers is to help our children know and experience the love of their heavenly Father. Yes, this is done when we read Scripture to them and talk to them about the Lord, but we also have the privilege and responsibility of modeling the love, discipline, forgiveness, and grace of God as well.

This is no small task. We must somehow learn to create an environment that resembles the spiritual truths at work in the gospel story. Of course, we need to teach our children there are consequences for sinful choices, but we also need to show them through the actions of our love that "if we confess our sins, he is faithful and just to forgive us our sins and to cleanse us from all unrighteousness" (1 John 1:9). This example means confession, and asking forgiveness restores relationship with the Father and should also restore relationship with us as well. As a matter of fact, we should be longing to forgive our children and restore them to relationship. That practice looks like God and paints the picture of the gospel story in real time.

Sometimes this practicing of the gospel means my child is the one who needs to admit sin, repent of it, and make a game plan to turn from it. Part of this means teaching my child how to say "I'm sorry" and mean it. I can't be the only one who has looked her child in the eye and said, "You need to tell your brother you're sorry," only to have him mutter the words under his breath and know that those words were not a turning of his heart but only external obedience. In no way was the child owning the weight of his error. This kind of apology does not meet the expectation of the Lord and fails to satisfy a human heart that needs to forgive. It leaves all of us unsatisfied, and rightfully so. Apologies should have three components:

1. We must *identify the sin* or injury and why it doesn't meet the standard of God.
2. We must *express sorrow* for injuring the other.
3. We must express a desire to *make another choice* in the future.

> The best way to teach children forgiveness is to go first.

This pattern, my friend, is how we say a good "I'm sorry," and in terms of biblical truth this is the anatomy of true repentance. When we repent before the Lord, we come clean about our sin, own the truth that it has harmed our relationship, and consciously make a choice to head in the direction of the behavior and attitudes pleasing to the Lord.

The best way to teach children forgiveness is to go first. I want my kids to say, "Yes, my mom taught me how to ask for and give forgiveness, but the way she modeled it is what stands out in my mind. She gave me a safe opportunity to learn how to forgive by asking me often for forgiveness when she fell short."

I recently heard Robert Wolgemuth and Nancy DeMoss Wolge-muth talking about racing to the cross of Christ. In their marriage, "go first" when it comes to admitting wrong has become part of their language. Robert said,

> In my humanity, I'd rather have you go first and have you come to me and say, "Robert, that just wasn't the right thing for me to say." Well, guess what? You may not see it that way, so I have to go first...I say, "Nancy, we need to talk. I would love to just tell you what's on my heart." Rarely in any human relationship (and certainly not in our marriage) are you disappointed when you go first. People love transparency. People love to welcome a person who comes to them in humility and repentance.
>
> Nancy quickly added, "Humility breeds humil-ity...That's where a wife can go first. And how motivat-ing that is to a man—to her husband, to a dad, to sons when there's a mom, a wife in the home who is taking that place."[1]

Isn't that what we are looking to instill in our children? Humility says, "I've done something wrong and I need forgiveness."

In this metaphor of racing to the cross of Christ, the primary ben-efit is a clear heart before the Lord, and the second is the by-product of modeling the gospel. We can race to Jesus, and the offer there is an unlimited well of forgiveness for ourselves and stronger relation-ships with our kids.

Home is a place of forgiveness,
and that starts with me.

The benefits to asking forgiveness extend beyond relieving the weight of sinful behavior. By asking our children for forgiveness, we are cultivating in them the idea that home is the place where it is okay to fail and try again. Even if you blow it, arms will be open to receive you. Home should be the safest place for our children to err and be restored. This is the place where it is safe for them to learn that procrastination doesn't pay, that electronics need monitoring, that money requires stewardship, and that harsh words can't be taken back. We want to create in advance a place where our children quickly admit their wrongdoing, so if they hit a hard patch as they grow, they know they still have a place to go.

One question we have used to cultivate this has been, "What do you wish you could do over today?" Sometimes the answers relate to relationships, and sometimes they are merely wishing we had slept longer and made better choices. The whole idea is that we are working together to build our strengths and support each other in our weaknesses, and to come home. Home is a place of forgiveness, and that starts with me.

Myths Debunked

Rarely are sticky situations and conversations one-sided. Often a holdout in my heart thinks if I apologize first my children could think they did nothing wrong. That might be true in your heart as well. That viewpoint, however, as real as it may feel, is askew and prevents grace from flowing through our lives into the situation. Admitting I was wrong doesn't let my child off the hook. It lets me off God's hook, and that is infinitely more important. Unconfessed sin toward someone else stops up what God wants to do in and through me.

Last night I just had to test the theory on a real audience. Mike was working late bringing in the corn harvest on the farm, and formalities fly out the window during this season. Dinner involved Doritos as a side dish. All four kids were home, and so after the perfunctory, "How was your day and what were its highs?" I told them about the topic at hand. I asked them, "Guys, do you think parents should ask their kids to forgive them?" All four of them looked at me as though I had grown four heads. Ryan, my littlest, looked right at me and said, "Well, yeah."

"How come, bud?"

"Because parents aren't perfect and God tells you to say 'I'm sorry.' And the Bible says, 'Children obey your parents in the Lord.'"

I laughed at his quick response and asked what children obeying their parents had to do with parents asking forgiveness. The whole crew jumped on board and explained to me that if kids had to obey parents, then parents better obey God. Makes sense to me.

> Vulnerability coupled with humility can set us up for a powerful infusion of Christ's strength.

I explained that some parents think saying they're sorry might lead their kids to feel less respect for their parents. This seemed ludicrous to all of them. In fact, that's when Brendan said, "Mom, when you ask for forgiveness we respect you even more."

They know when we're doing it wrong, friends. Just like we know when they are getting it wrong, they sense when we are out of step with the Lord. We must somehow rid ourselves of the idea that vulnerability equals weakness. Vulnerability coupled with humility can set us up for a powerful infusion of Christ's strength. Scripture is crystal clear about this: "God opposes the proud but gives grace to the humble" (James 4:6).

It just figures, doesn't it? When we humble ourselves before our children, we become stronger leaders, not weaker.

I have for years taken exception to King David's response to his sin with Bathsheba. Psalm 51 is a template for us of a repentant heart, and we are told in the notes before the psalm that it was written when the prophet Nathan came to David after he committed adultery with Bathsheba and orchestrated the death of her husband, Uriah. It begins well enough.

> Have mercy on me, O God, according to your unfailing love; according to your great compassion blot out my transgressions. Wash away all my iniquity and cleanse me

from my sin. For I know my transgressions, and my sin
is always before me. Against you, you only, have I sinned
and done what is evil in your sight (Psalm 51:1-4 NIV).

Call me crazy, but I'm pretty sure he had sinned against more than
just the Lord. Although I know the heart of what he's saying here
is that the most grievous infraction was against God, David sinned
against Uriah, Bathsheba, and the country he led as well, not to mention the children he already had for whom he was setting a tragic
example. A wise pastor once told me the scope of the apology should
match the scope of the offense, and I wholeheartedly believe our children should be included in our apologies when they are injured by
our poor choices.

Search Me

You know the kind of day you wish would just end? You can't
believe it's happening, and you wonder if a hidden camera is somewhere close. I feel as though I have more than my fair share of those
days as a mom of four and a farm wife. However, one day will live in
infamy.

It all began as I was combing my daughter's lovely, thick hair. I was
parting it when I looked down and thought I saw a bug in her hair. I
quickly grabbed it and set it on the bathroom counter, and that was
when panic swept over me. I grabbed my smartphone and quickly
typed, "What do lice look like?" The tiny picture that appeared was
the twin of the crawling thing on my counter. I thought I might die.
I pulled back another strip of hair with the comb, and there before
me was another twin.

If you find lice on your daughter, you should know some things.
First, it would be best to cancel any plans you have for the next three
weeks, because you will be shampooing, combing, washing, vacuum-
ing, and freaking out for a while. Second, odds are terrific your other
children also have it. And third, it is totally appropriate to cry your

eyes out. At least, those are the things that happened here. I found lice on both girls that morning before school and immediately stripped the beds, only momentarily considering lighting a match to their whole room, not that I'm dramatic. That day I spent from 8:00 a.m. until 5:00 p.m. cleaning and doing laundry, and nit-picking, quite literally. It took me over four hours to de-nit one daughter that day, and that, my friend, is not an exaggeration. When Mike came home from work and found me rocking in my closet (not really—but close), I told him my head had been itching since I found the first louse that morning. Sure enough, upon further review, I discovered I had lice as well.

I sat on the floor before my husband, begging him to be thorough. "Please, look close, you can't miss even one. Is that light good enough? Can you see everything?" Humiliated and weary, I began to see a spiritual parallel between lice and sin. I was reminded of Psalm 139:23-24.

> Search me, O God, and know my heart! Try me and know
> my thoughts! And see if there be any grievous way in me,
> and lead me in the way everlasting.

Sin always separates us from the Lord and the ones we love. Lice are skilled at multiplying, but any sin left unchecked and unaddressed in us is even more poisonous. What did King David believe about God that caused him to lay his heart before the Lord and beg Him to search through it? Undoubtedly he had faced agonizing shame and destruction when sin festered in his heart or he would not have reached this place of desperation. What I find most comforting, though, is his obvious belief that God would still love him, forgive him, and restore him during and after the process.

One commentator says the "grievous way" could be translated "the way of pain."[2] It seems obvious to me that, when we ask God to search our hearts, we are asking Him to take us off the path that leads to pain in us and our children and set our feet on a different path. This searching starts inside us. It begins with one BRAVE mom humbling herself before the Lord and asking Him to search her and see if anything needs to be addressed.

We need the Lord to search our hearts in two key areas. The first involves distraction, and the second, inconsistency.

Distraction

"Many parents are with their children physically, but mentally their focus is elsewhere. Togetherness without genuine encounter is not togetherness at all."[3] Dorothy Briggs wrote those words in 1970, and I have to wonder what she would think about the distractions that avail themselves to parents today. Dorothy was writing to a generation that was distracted by television when, unless you left the room, you had to watch commercials. Today, we watch television on demand without commercials, or at least have the ability to fast-forward through them. We carry the worldwide web in our back pockets or our purses, and no one sits by their radios to record a song onto a cassette tape; we pull it up on our phones whenever we want.

Honestly, I love being a part of this generation for this reason. I have a list app on my phone, I can set reminders to take treats to an event on my phone, I text my friends on my phone, I listen to sermons on my phone, and I can read the Bible on my phone. All those are great things that can enhance my life, but as for most other parents, it is easy for me to be swept away for 15 minutes or an hour at a time. I cannot, however, divide my attention between my screen and my children. I've tried.

This is a gut check of epic proportions. It's not unusual to find our family huddled up for family movie night with me surfing Pinterest, uninvolved in memory making, or checking my phone when it dings during dinner. I've left a room only to have my children bring me my phone because I'd forgotten to carry it with me as if it were a part of my body. At best, I'm numbing out of life by staying distracted and not present in the moment with my kids. At worst,

I'm avoiding doing the job I've been called to do. This doesn't mean I can't have a phone, but it does mean I must remember this is my season to have genuine, life-shaping encounters with my children and that I have a problem that needs attention. This is just one more area that leads me to repentance before the Lord and my children. Further, I could probably use a little accountability from someone invested in my process.

My apology to my kids is going to sound like this: "Honeys, I'm sorry I've been distracted by my phone when you've needed my attention. I'm trying to learn how to have healthy boundaries in this area, and I want you to be able to have them too. I haven't always gotten this right, but I want you to know I love you and I want to show you that by limiting the time I'm distracted while we're together. Will you forgive me?"

I do want my kids to have healthy boundaries when it comes to social media, television, video games, and all the rest. I pray my apology sets the tone for the standards we will build into our home.

Inconsistency

Inconsistency in parenting leaves children guessing about what the expectation will be. One of the things we're probably most grateful for is the absolute consistency of God. We've already discussed this at some length, but we can praise God that His standard for us never changes, nor does His commitment to our refining process wane. We have a great tendency to be both hot and cold when it comes to disciplining and discipling our children.

For example, we can enter a season of particular stress at work, a busy sports schedule, or the holidays and allow routines and healthy boundaries to slip. We can allow poor interpersonal habits to develop in our kids that grow seemingly overnight, or we can just be too tired to discipline. We will all experience some of the above, or all the above at one point or another. When this happens, instead of continuing to allow the slide to occur, we must apologize for the inconsistency in us, explain how the failure on our part to follow through has harmed our children, ask for forgiveness, and begin again.

Parents of teenagers might be tempted to believe the time they have left is not sufficient to accomplish the task of raising a hero of the faith. This is a lie—a powerful lie from the enemy of our souls. No situation is ever too far gone for Christ to redeem. This means you can breathe a sigh of relief right now, understanding that although you will face an uphill battle, God is on your side. God is unable to resist those who humble themselves before Him, ask for His forgiveness, and beg for Him to intervene. Today is the day to start again. Today is the day to ask the Lord for forgiveness and to ask your child for forgiveness. I imagine that conversation would sound a little like this:

"I need to ask you to forgive me. I haven't set a standard for you that is godly, and I've been passive when it came to teaching you _____. Please forgive me. I've prayed and asked the Lord for help. I believe the habits you've been building are going to need some tweaking, and I'm committed to helping you adjust those so they meet God's standard. I'm committed to obeying the Lord and helping you learn to obey Him too. I love you."

I don't think for a moment that a conversation with our children, confessing and addressing our inconsistency, will be easy. Far from it. I won't always be consistent in my emotional responses or in my discipline of my children. I can't even be consistent in getting dinner on the table. But this I know: if I confess it, He forgives it, and we begin again.

Prison Ministry

Charles Colson is the perfect example of a parent who failed miserably. Chuck had a brilliant mind, a hard-work ethic, and a love for politics. He married young and began a family that included two boys and a beautiful baby girl. His determined spirit made him invaluable at work, but scarcely available at home. He soon had an exciting career as an attorney, campaign strategist, and finally special counsel for the president at the young age of 38. Like many of us who allow ourselves to be career focused yet family blind, this drive for success in the workplace cost Chuck his first marriage. Although he loved his kids dearly, his time with them was brief.

Even after marrying the woman he would spend the rest of his life with, Patty, Chuck found success in the world of Washington, D.C., and politics. His driven spirit made him an asset to Richard Nixon's 1968 and 1972 presidential campaigns. He wrote, "Being a part of electing a president was the fondest ambition of my life. For three long years I had committed everything I had, every ounce of energy to Richard Nixon's cause. Nothing else had mattered. We had no time together as a family, no social life, no vacations."[4]

At work, Chuck's loyalty to the president and to power took over and he became President Nixon's ruthless right-hand man. Soon ethical compromises led him to places he could scarcely imagine. Lost in his lust for power, he began contriving situations, mutilating reputations, and ruthlessly dealing with enemies of the Nixon administration. He is perhaps most notorious for his participation in the Watergate scandal that shocked and dismayed the nation. Charges were brought against him, and his entire family faced the consequences of his ruthless political behavior.

Describing this time in their lives, Chuck wrote, "Through all of this, the children proved their mettle, especially when my world collapsed and I was embroiled in the Watergate scandal. They paid an especially high price, often being mocked by other kids. And one day the teacher in Emily's high school class spoke about what an evil man Charles Colson was."[5]

In the spring of 1974, official charges were brought against Chuck for conspiracy in the cover-up of the Watergate burglaries. What followed was an agonizing season for Chuck and his family, and that's when God led a friend to share with him the good news of Christ and a copy of C. S. Lewis's *Mere Christianity*. Chuck cried out to God to save him in August of 1974, and the trajectory of his life began to change.

Although life-altering legal pressures loomed, Chuck studied his new faith with the heart of an attorney. Believers on both sides of the political aisle reached out to him as brothers in Christ, encouraging him amid career devastation. Chuck's pride was publicly being dismantled day by day, but his inner man was growing with each day. As the charges pressed forward and revealed the ugliness of his old self, he acknowledged that although he was not guilty of all the charges against him, he was guilty of some. Ultimately, he pled guilty to obstruction of justice and served seven months in an Alabama prison.

Although the change in Chuck was real and deep, it did not stop hurt and devastation from sweeping over his family. At one point his bright and friendly 18-year-old son, Chris, was arrested for narcotics possession and jailed. Chris told the officers, "Now you've got both of us." Can you imagine the heartbreak of his newly Christ-following father?[6]

Only God can write a story with the depth of redemption Chuck Colson experienced. God restored their family over time, and Chuck went on to become one of the most influential believers in Christendom. God used that brilliant mind and tireless work ethic to form an international prison ministry, to write more than 30 books defending the faith, and to develop a radio broadcast helping Americans navigate the challenges of faith. God used that born-again man's greatest failure to change the world.

In December 2015, Colson's son Chris wrote the following:

> My dad's incarceration was tough. His case had been national news, so all of my friends knew where he was—and why. When I went to visit him, a prison-issue uniform had replaced his usual coat and tie. He answered to a prison number instead of prestigious titles that had graced him in the past. He was even gone for Christmas.

In spite of the difficulties, I can say with the benefit of hindsight that my dad's prison sentence was the best thing that happened to him and our family. Instead of a curse, it was a gift. My dad had to lose almost everything in order to become a new person—the father and husband God intended him to be. And God didn't just use my father's scandal and incarceration to bless our immediate family; because of the time he served...God's love, grace, and truth have transformed countless lives.[7]

Never, ever believe your mistakes can't be forgiven or healed. We serve a God who takes parental failures and rebuilds families, sometimes even moving the kingdom of God forward as He does. When all is said and done, we must trust that God will take the crummy choices we've made and even our greatest defeats and failures and use them to give our kids a future and hope, and to build dynamic faith.

Lord,
I trust You to show me areas of my life, attitudes, and actions that need to be addressed. Search me, know my heart and my thoughts, and show me what I need to see. I know of areas where You desire growth inside me in relationship with my kids. Forgive me for being distracted in times my kids have truly needed me and for the times I'm using media to numb out. I want my priorities to be Yours, so teach me how to set healthy boundaries on my time. I also want to enjoy the time I spend with my kids. Please give me creativity and a sense of humor to delight in the gifts You have given me in my children. I invite You to work in our family and I ask You to start in me. Amen.

9

Vigilant Prayer

*I remember my mother's prayers and they have always
followed me. They have clung to me all my life.*
—Abraham Lincoln

I could get comfortable only on the roof. Even though the sun had
set hours before, the heat inside the house was suffocating. Haiti in
August is a thing. It was impossible to get air to blow through the mission house no matter how you tried to move the two fans that ran
when the generator had gas. We figured a conservative guess had the
inside of the house a sweltering 100 degrees.

Mike and I were in Port-au-Prince, working with 30 women's and
children's ministry coordinators from five different churches. We had
worked so hard to get ready for the conference, cleaning the mission
house top to bottom from the dust that had accumulated from being
shut up for months at a time and from the dust that comes up off the
road every time a car drives by. Haiti was already the poorest country in the Western Hemisphere before the earthquake that decimated
it on January 12, 2010. Many of the streets still looked like a snow-
plow went through the center and threw the debris to the sides, with
enough room for a car to get through but not cleaned up enough to
forget.

As we were getting ready for bed the first evening, I turned to the team leader and said, "I can't sleep like this. It is *so* hot." I was dripping with sweat and couldn't imagine sleeping in a room with Mike and another couple with no windows. Just the idea was agony. I asked if it would be possible to carry our mattresses up to the flat roof of the house so we could at least get the Caribbean breeze.

The problem was not the logistics of carrying all four mattresses to the roof—we were willing to do anything to make this possible. The problem was convincing our security team it was a safe decision. It's quite possible to jump from roof to roof in Port-au-Prince. Our security guards could not believe we crazy Americans wanted to do it, but they finally consented. As we laid our sweaty, exhausted, and culture-shocked heads on those pillows that first night, I wondered what on earth I was doing there.

While the breeze blew over us at a perfect 80 degrees, it began to dawn on me that although we were no longer sweltering, the air was filled with unfamiliar noises, shouts, car sounds, music, and twice that first night, gunshots. I rolled over and looked at my girlfriend Jeanna when I heard the first shot, and she peered back and questioningly made a gun sign with her fingers. I nodded and then rolled the other way and nudged Mike. "Honey, I heard a gunshot!" He mumbled a sleepy, "Okay," and then fell back to sleep. I, however, would find no rest that night—or the next. I would lie awake and listen to this singing and chanting, the shrieks of laughter and car horns, exhausted but unable to adapt.

My heart was breaking and learning to love in a way I had never known during the day, but at night I wrestled with this growing rage that it was so hot and so loud. The noises were still startling and scary. A disco club blocks away emitted a pulsing techno beat. And then the singing and chanting. Who were the people singing and chanting, and why couldn't they stop?

Finally, one evening I crawled onto the end of Hannah and Cephas's bed and said, "Cephas, what is that chanting?"

He listened and then joined the rhythmic chant with his own

deep voice. "It's Scripture, Lee," he said. "They are reciting Scripture, singing praise and worshiping and praying. The women of the church have a lock-in and fast and pray all night and into the morning." When I returned to my own bed, I pondered what he'd told me and wondered if I had ever prayed for more than an hour at a time in my whole life.

A few years ago, we had a ladies' retreat speaker at the Christian camp where I frequently serve. During the Saturday morning session, I was sitting with my mentor, Meltha, and a few other dynamos in the kingdom of God. If I were to pick a team to head into spiritual battle, these women would be my army commanders. Meltha is the kind of woman who leaves you feeling as though you've spent time with Jesus. Her speech is permeated with Scripture, and when she says she'll pray for you, you will know you've been carried to the throne.

We listened to the speaker talk about how prayer had been an important part of the change in her life. I'm sure we nodded our heads in agreement, because, well, of course. At this point, I've walked with Jesus long enough to know the ability to communicate in real time with Him is the greatest privilege and power source we have. Then the speaker asked, "Who in this room is a prayer warrior? Go on— raise your hands."

I'm not kidding, my first thought was, "I am *not* a prayer warrior. I know prayer warriors, but I would not say that about myself." And in that moment I hung my head in shame. Although I serve five counties as the Area Coordinator for Moms in Prayer International and I pray all the time, I know my prayer life has much more room for improvement. Besides, I was sitting beside my mentor, who is a legitimate intercessor.

As the speaker called those prayer warriors to the front of the room, I pondered the importance of that calling and the shame I felt, fully expecting the seat next to me to be vacated. But Meltha stayed seated right next to me.

Later, one of my closest friends, Abby, asked me why I didn't go to the front of the room; the speaker had been looking for people willing to pray with others. I told her, "I couldn't. I have so far to go in that area." In my heart I knew I was a wimpy warrior.

What was telling to me, though, was not the condition of my heart, but rather what happened with my mentor. Meltha doesn't think she has arrived as a vigilant prayer warrior either. Praise God someone went forward to pray with others, but what rattled me that day was this awareness that it would be super easy for us to continue to stay in our seats, feeling defeated in the area of prayer.

Finding Our Footing

> Arise, cry out in the night, at the beginning of the night watches! Pour out your heart like water before the presence of the Lord! Lift your hands to him for the lives of your children, who faint for hunger at the head of every street (Lamentations 2:19).

We want to and we know we need to pray, so why is prayer so difficult? We're told to pray continually and to give thanks in all circumstances. We're told to pray according to the will of God and to do it without doubting. But sometimes I want to whisper, "You know I have children, right, Lord?" I squandered my uninterrupted time before children and now uninterrupted time seems impossible to find. Maybe you, too, feel as though you're failing in the area of prayer and you are covered in shame.

Allow the Spirit to lift your head in this sacred moment.

He knows.

He knows our limitations. He hears the static in our minds as we approach Him. He cares that we feel inept. He's in it neck-deep with us, friend. We must simply choose to stand up again, to war through prayer.

We know opposition to our humbling ourselves before the Lord, because the Enemy wins if we are prayer-less. But oh, if we knew the full ramifications of a vigilant, praying mother! There is no fiercer warrior than a mama whose child is in harm's way. We must cast aside the peacetime mentality that easily blinds us and see the reality stretched out in front of us. Today, right now, we face a raging battle.

> We do not wrestle against flesh and blood, but against the rulers, against the authorities, against the cosmic powers over this present darkness, against the spiritual forces of evil in the heavenly places. Therefore take up the whole armor of God, that you may be able to withstand in the evil day, and having done all, to stand firm...praying at all times in the Spirit, with all prayer and supplication (Ephesians 6:12-13,18).

With the increasing ferocity of the Enemy in our generation, and with his nasty strategy of picking on our children, attacking our marriages, and deceiving the people we love, we cannot afford to be wimpy prayer warriors. We must become vigilant in every way, recognizing that the way through is to stand firmly in the power of Christ and pray, pray, pray.

We will find our footing in prayer as we build our prayer strategy:

WANT TO

LEARN TO

DEVELOP IT

SCHEDULE IT

WANT TO: *Asking for a Vigilant Spirit*

To gain success in the area of prayer, we must fan into a flame the hunger for prayer inside us. Sometimes our *want to* is broken. *I don't want to wake up early. I don't want to ask for the Lord's will if I don't know what it is. I don't enjoy it.* Do you believe, precious friend, that God could grow the *want to* inside you? If we ask anything according to His will He grants that prayer in Christ. Let's make this one our prayer.

> Father,
> I'm grateful for the privilege and right I have as Your child to approach You through prayer. I'm grateful for Christ, who inter-cedes for me right now. I'm asking You to create in me a hunger for prayer and intercession. I want to want to. My children need me to pray, and if I'm not doing this job, who will? The responsibility to intercede for my children is indeed mine. I love them. Teach me to cry out fervently and frequently on their behalf. Make me a vigilant, praying mama, I ask in Jesus's name. Amen.

LEARN TO: *Becoming a Student of Prayer*

Recently, out of curiosity, I counted the books within arm's reach that exclusively deal with the matter of prayer. I counted 16. Sixteen. And I have more on my nightstand and on shelves throughout our home. I love them, savor them, and learn from them, but I can honestly say the greatest lesson in prayer has come from an entirely different source.

My education in prayer hit Masters level when my head knowledge became experiential as I gathered with other mothers to pray with through Moms in Prayer International. You don't amass 16 books on prayer unless the *want to* has been cultivated in you by the Holy Spirit. Some fantastic biographies have been written about passionate pray-ers, and Scripture is filled with examples of God's children who stood in the gap for their generation. As you read about them, take notes. Lean in as you read.

I love listening to others pray, and I love trying new things and keeping this area fresh, but mostly I am amazed that God invites us and beckons us to come. He demands no one method of prayer, but simply this invitation to come.

> Truly, truly, I say to you, whatever you ask of the Father in my name, he will give it to you. Until now you have asked nothing in my name. Ask, and you will receive, that your joy may be full (John 16:23-24).

DEVELOP IT: Using a Prayer Strategy

Prayer is a muscle you strengthen. Listen, anytime we pray is a good time. The Lord knows we need Him all the time for a myriad of moment-to-moment reasons, and so we are told to pray continually. Experience tells me, however, that developing vigilance in prayer takes time and focus.

A good place to begin is to schedule a time to work at this, somewhere you can have some privacy. Heaven knows this can be difficult! I sometimes feel my children have an alarm system wired from my Bible to their internal clocks, because whenever I make it to the couch to meet with the Lord in the mornings, they inevitably wake up. That's life, folks, but we're looking for progress. Then focus on developing a workable, simple plan for the week. Is it ten minutes in the morning when you pray for yourself, your spouse if you have one, your child, and then last for a rotating list of family members who need the Lord? As I pray down my system, I've found stamina in prayer growing and time beginning to pass more quickly. The goal is not time logged in, but rather the connection with the Father and an earnest desire for Him to work.

One of the most important parts of developing a prayer strategy is learning how to pray Scripture over our children and claim the promises God has made to us and to them. Any Scripture can become a prayer. One of my favorite things to do is pray psalms back to the Lord and over my children. For example, Psalm 143:8 says, "Let me hear in the morning of your steadfast love, for in you I trust. Make me know the way I should go, for to you I lift up my soul." This quickly turns into a prayer for anyone when we substitute his or her name: "Let Gabriella hear in the morning of Your steadfast love, for in You she trusts. Make Gabriella know the way she should go as she lifts her soul to You."

When I pray my words, I try to fill them with truth. But when I pray Scripture, I know I'm praying powerfully and effectively.

SCHEDULE IT: Making Prayer a Part of the Fabric of Your Life

Prayer begets prayer. The more you pray, the more you want to pray and the more answers you see. I've developed prayer rhythms into my day that help prompt me to pray.

- Before my feet hit the floor in the morning, I ask the Lord to direct my day and commit myself to be His hands and feet.
- I spend time in the Word and then use a resource that helps me pray over each child about a godly characteristic I'd like to see grow and develop. I keep track of those characteristics in a notebook.
- When we back out of the garage for school, I pray for each of the kids' teachers and principals and ask for my kids to be change agents in their classrooms.
- Once a week I meet with my Moms in Prayer group and pray with my friends over our kids, the teachers, and strategically for the needs in our district.
- I pray for several places in our community each time I drive by them.
- Every night before we go to sleep, Mike and I pray again over our family, our friends, and often for our nation. Mike's strategy is similar to mine, except his responsibilities include bedtime prayer requests with the kids. He asks for the concerns of their hearts and then prays with them and for them.

These are hard stops throughout the day when prayer for our family and community are built in. They are rhythms built into the fabric of my life. As you probably suspect, because we've become convinced that God is listening and answering, we've been spurred on to try to add even more stops throughout the day. Prayer has now permeated our home and my life, and it doesn't feel like an area of defeat at all. It's living and breathing and is becoming something our home is known for.

A Broken-Down City

Jerusalem lay in shambles. The king of Babylon had long ago demolished the land. He looted the temple and hauled off Judah's sons and daughters. He burned the house of God and the royal palaces and broke down the walls of the city. Decades later, the children of Israel were still living in captivity, waiting for the day the Lord would end their exile.

Although they were being disciplined severely, the Lord still loved them and had chosen them to be His treasured possession. The book of Ezra tells us God stirred up the spirit of a foreign king, Cyrus, to allow His people to return home and rebuild the temple of Jerusalem.

You'd think everyone would want to go. You'd think everyone would be ready for a little freedom. But just like complacency and contentment with the status quo lulls our generation to sleep, so the exiled Jews did not all dart for the door.

In their defense, they knew the journey would be hard, and once they arrived they'd face uncertain living conditions, hard labor, dangerous enemies, and a task that would require every bit of their energy and concentration. (It just sounds so much like motherhood.)

Once the exiles who did go arrived, they must have surveyed the ruins. I can readily picture the older, weary travelers standing in front of the wreck that used to be their home. Imagine sifting through a place you abandoned in an emergency 44 years earlier. That was the situation the exiles came home to.

Year one was survival. Shelter, food, fire—the basics.

Year two, Ezra tells us, they had cleared the rubble and laid the foundation for the new temple. When the builders stood back and surveyed their work, the priests and the singers led the people in praise to the Lord. But something peculiar was happening simultaneously,

> Many of the priests and Levites and heads of fathers' houses, old men who had seen the first house, wept with a loud voice when they saw the foundation of this house being laid, though many shouted aloud for joy, so that the people could not distinguish the sound of the joyful shout from the sound of the people's weeping, for the people shouted with a great shout, and the sound was heard far away (Ezra 3:12-13).

The young exiles returned to the land eager to work and rebuild a homeland they didn't remember or yet know, while the older generation wept in dismay at the conditions of the heritage and temple they loved. Life would never be the same. They both were right.

We can't miss this moment because it is happening today, and perhaps has happened in many generations of the past. The same tension exists within *our* homes and in churches. Life is not the same. Gone are the days when we left kids in the car unattended, gone are the days when we prayed in our schools, gone seem to be the days when faith was expected and virtue esteemed. Some look back over their shoulders and legitimately long for the way things were. That time seemed wholesome, safe, and right.

But we must not paint the past with perfection. Although Jerusalem was home to the temple of the living God and they were free to practice their faith in God complete with the sacrifices and worship services He prescribed, the Jewish people were still led astray. During the times of peace people's hearts were most adrift. Likewise, as we glance at history over our shoulders, it is necessary to see that, while only a generation ago people would have more readily identified themselves as believers, what resulted was a cultural Christianity rather than the faith that transformed homes. Just as the young returning exiles returned to a land different from the one their fathers knew, we face a new and different cultural landscape in which we will parent. The last thing in the world we need to do while our children are worshiping our God is to sit wailing for what was. These are the conditions they have been given. And what they are singing is right. "He is good, for his steadfast love endures forever" (Ezra 3:11).

Then there was the matter of the enemies in the land. When God allowed the northern kingdom of Israel to fall to Assyria, it was not enough for the people to be carried off. The king of Assyria resettled the land of Israel with people from Mesopotamia and Aram. The few Israelites who remained were overtaken with false religions and foreign gods. Some of those who settled in the land embraced parts of the worship of the Lord. As the exiles from Babylon returned to the land, these foreigners who had moved in while they were away were concerned. They were determined to see the rebuilders discouraged and afraid, bribing people to frustrate their plans. As the next wave of exiles returned under a new king, the road to Jerusalem became even more dangerous, and the people would be called to fast and pray for protection from the enemy. Who but the Lord could reroute the enemy, cloak the exiles in safety, and bring them to their land?

Sometimes the path to the place God calls our children is not freshly paved. I have watched God call my friends and family members into places where no physical safety was assured. They have been exactly where God wanted them. Prayer and fasting seem altogether appropriate in these times—as well as when their physical safety may not be in question but their spiritual safety is up in the air.

During this time God raised up men to lead the people. One was Ezra, a priest and scribe living in exile who had found favor with the Lord and the foreign king, "for the good hand of his God was on him" (Ezra 7:9). Ezra returned to Jerusalem and found the people of God living in sin and disobedience. His response showed his heart: he wept, tore his cloak, and led the way in confession, weeping, and prayer.

And Ezra wasn't the only one distraught over the sin of Jerusalem and the exiles. Back in Babylon, God was raising up another tender yet strong leader. Nehemiah was a man of deep prayer, and he asked the Lord to hear his night and day prayers.

Nehemiah soon joined the exiles in Jerusalem with the mission of rebuilding the city walls. He was met with the same disheartening conditions, the same rubble, the same enemies. How did Nehemiah respond? With prayer, but also with diligence in the work. When enemies loomed large, he set a watch over the workers and put them in shifts. He never allowed the watch to end or lapse. When it was time to rebuild, the people rebuilt the portion of the wall right in front of their homes. Why? Because no one would do a better job building a secure wall than the one who would live directly behind it.

Ruminate for a while on the similarities of the ruins, political landscape, and spiritual climate that met the exiles in Jerusalem and the world we are raising our children in today.

Mama, I love your child. I do. I really do. And even as I write these words I am asking for the Lord to build a hedge around your family and to raise mighty warriors in the kingdom of God from your lineage. I pray you will be strong and courageous for the task ahead, and that like Nehemiah's, your hands will be strong for the task.

But really, friend, no one will do a better job rebuilding the spiritual walls around your child, home, and community than you. No one. Half the battle is beginning. This is your time. Take your stand.

Father,
I praise You for being the God who hears and listens when I call. What a privilege You have offered me, the opportunity and right to bring my joys and concerns before You. Forgive me for the times I've chosen to fret about what concerns my children instead of interceding for them. Create in me a heart for prayer and teach me how to build new prayer habits. I want Your direction and will for our family. In Jesus's name, amen.

10

Equip Them

Moral excellence comes about as a result of habit. We become just by doing just acts, temperate by doing temperate acts, brave by doing brave acts.

—ARISTOTLE

I was breathing in the clean scent of her hair when I asked my daughter Lexie Beth the question.

Mike and I had prayerfully made the decision to homeschool our entire tribe for one year. Prayerful is the only way you can make the decision to take on a responsibility that large, and at the end of the year we had stacks of notebooks full of work, piles of books we had read together, and a closer family. It was worth it—not easy, but worth it. We were also prayerfully making the decision to return them to school, and public school at that. I was apprehensive about what influences we would unknowingly be inviting into our kids' lives and secretly wondered if we would lose the growth we'd seen in them. But I wouldn't be sharing any of that on this particular morning.

"Lexie, honey, are you excited to go to school next week?"

Lexie Beth is the spitting image of her mother, or at least that's what people tell me. She looked at me, and then softly said, "Yeah, Mama. But I sure am going to miss hearing about Jesus." Tears stung my eyes—they still do as I recall that moment. Something in me rose up in that moment. I know it was the Holy Spirit, but I'd also like to think it was bravery.

"No, baby girl. That's my job. I'm the one who will be teaching you about Jesus. You will get out of the van in the morning and I will be saying the name of Jesus over you, and you will get back in in the afternoon and I will be saying His name. That's my job."

The minute we think we can hand that responsibility to a school, a daycare employee, a coach, or even a youth pastor, we have it wrong. Training our kids to love and follow Christ is our job, Mama. There is no substitute for a mother's tender training to win her child's heart to Christ. God has a special anointing available just for this role.

The Huns Are Coming

The work of transformation astounds me. From the hatching of tadpoles in the creek behind our home all the way to their losing their tails and crawling out of the water, I love it. Did you know a gillion tadpoles that hatch never become anything else? They just die in a tad-pole state. The ones that do make it are real fighters, overcomers. (One time I touched a frog that still had a tail. It was weird. Really weird.)

I'm not sure if it's just me, or if others enjoy watching development too. I geek out on movies that show lead characters becoming fight-ers, or gaining self-discipline, or performing the very best they are capable of, overcoming incredible odds to do so. Overcoming is what we were made to do. Before we send warriors out into battle expect-ing them to advance the kingdom of God, however, they need to be equipped and trained.

One scene in the animated film *Mulan* shows this little girl rid-ing off into battle, answering her father's call to service in the Chi-nese army. Mulan fears the loss of her father more than she fears the battle that awaits. She gets pummeled in the beginning of basic training and is exhausted and defeated, but as the Disney music cre-scendos, she finds her stride and learns to master the skills and weap-ons she's been given, not the least of which is her mind. She saves her commander (and all of China) before being discovered as a woman. I love that stuff.

A Word of Warning

Before we dive into Part Three of this book, I want to issue a strong word of caution. Sally Michael sums it up this way:

> Though our calling is a serious calling which we must work at faithfully, we must remember that our diligent efforts will not save our children; they may be the means God uses to save our children, but we do not have the power to change their hearts.[1]

Our efforts must be infused with the Holy Spirit or they will fall short. Some days we won't know how to train these children. We may try a thousand different methods, and perhaps some days we'll want to sell our kids on eBay. (Bad idea.) The good news is when we tap into the well of Christ Jesus, it will never run dry. The end of us is the beginning of Him.

> If anyone speaks, they should do so as one who speaks the very words of God. If anyone serves, they should do so with the strength God provides, so that in all things God may be praised through Jesus Christ. To him be the glory and the power for ever and ever. Amen (1 Peter 4:11 NIV).

Friends, at the end of the day, we do our best and entrust our children to God. Remember? Surrender says, "I give up fighting." Entrust says, "Because of who You are, I choose to trust."

Trust and train. I like that.

Fighting—Like It or Not

I imagine that the Abar generation, the one that would leave the desert wanderings and take possession of the promised land, was a bit like you and me. Imagine them standing and listening to Moses as he spoke in the voice they had known since childhood. Hearing the age in his voice, they probably wondered to themselves how many times they had heard him say the same thing. But let's give them the benefit of the doubt and assume their hearts found a certain sweetness in hearing their leader tell them again the story about their parents' hasty departure from Egypt, the miracle at the Red Sea, the discipline in the desert, and the first time they tasted manna. Perhaps they felt the same warmth we feel when we hear someone we love repeat a story already told dozens of times.

Toward the end of my grandfather's life, I made the long trip to see my grandparents and Mom with my kids in tow. The path between Western Michigan and Northwest Arkansas is well worn by my frequent road trips. I am often the lone driver, stopping at nearly the same spots every trip. The first time I drove it alone, the only adult in the car, my extended family was a wreck, constantly calling to make sure I was okay. At the time I had two toddlers and a baby who napped quite a bit of the way, and I passed the miles reveling in the alone time in my own head, the Twizzlers I could secretly eat without sharing, and a book on tape—a break from one with illustrations.

Upon my arrival, everyone breathed a collective sigh of relief, but perhaps none like my grandparents. We had a great visit, and the night before I was to journey home with my little tribe, I sneaked over to their home alone to talk one last time. As we sat at their table, my grandfather, who was fading from Parkinson's disease, reminded me of the best way to get around St. Louis on the way home. Overflowing with love for me, he reminded me again that sometimes the best way is a little longer than the direct route. After he drew the path for me on a folded napkin, he circled the key interchange on the map he'd made.

This would be one of my very last memories of him before the Lord called him home—his fading voice, his shaky hands, and the love in his eyes as he showed me the way one more time.

So it was with Moses as the people prepared to leave the desert. If you have read the first few books of the Bible, then you know by the time you reach the book of Deuteronomy you have heard the story of the exodus many, many times. This time, however, as Moses reminds them of the past and twists in the road behind them, they lean forward because it's time for the trip to their new home. They have never traveled the path ahead, and they will go under new leadership without him.

Moses looks at them and lovingly says,

> If you will be careful to do all this commandment that I command you to do, loving the LORD your God, walking in all his ways, and holding fast to him, then the LORD will drive out all these nations before you, and you will dispossess nations greater and mightier than you (Deuteronomy 11:22-23).

Mike reminded me of the time when we took our family to a hockey game. Everyone was so excited to be there and the chill in the arena only fueled our excitement. The whistle blew, the puck dropped on the ice, and gloves immediately came flying off. Before we knew it a massive fight began right in front of us with grown men pounding on each other. Our kids were appalled. We had forgotten to tell them fights often take place in hockey, and this was a startling introduction to the game.

Friends, if we don't tell our kids that following Christ is going to be a fight, they will be shocked when the journey gets tough. Jesus told us, "I have said these things to you, that in me you may have peace. In the world you will have tribulation. But take heart; I have overcome the world" (John 16:33).

God told the Israelites there would be giants ahead. The land had enemies in it and they were the kind with fortified walls that seemed like giants. At times the path to victory would make no logical sense, and the only way to take the next step would be waiting on the Lord and obeying quickly. This land would be their children's inheritance, but it was up to them to claim and inhabit it. They had to drive out the enemy by the power of God and claim victory in His name. Little by little they would drive them out, and as they settled the promised land, they had to train their children diligently to obey the Lord.

> You shall therefore lay up these words of mine in your heart and in your soul, and you shall bind them as a sign on your hand, and they shall be as frontlets between your eyes. You shall teach them to your children, talking of them when you are sitting in your house, and when you are walking by the way, and when you lie down, and when you rise (Deuteronomy 11:18-19).

Oh, did we think those words were for only the Israelites? They're for us in this twenty-first century too. We have a land to take in front of us, and it's the one we're peering into. It's the one that may terrify us, that's wrought with enemies who threaten us with violence and corruption. It's a land filled with idols and traps that lure us into individuality and self-preservation. We can't misunderstand or forget for a minute that what lies ahead of us in raising the next generation of Christ followers will be a fight. But just like the Israelites, we fight from a place of victory because of the God on our side. Just as they had to work diligently to claim the land and train their children well, so must we.

Right before Moses's death, God calls him to the top of the mountain and shows him the promised land he will not enter. There He gives Moses one of his final assignments as the leader of God's people. "Charge Joshua, and encourage and strengthen him, for he shall go over at the head of this people, and he shall put them in possession of the land that you shall see" (Deuteronomy 3:28).

Charge

God tells Moses it's time to transfer the mantle of leadership to Joshua, to lay the responsibility on his shoulders to lead these people into the next season. This is our first step in equipping as well. One translation uses the word *commission*. When we commission someone, we charge him or her to accomplish a task or to enter service, and both are appropriate in this context. As we equip our children for the road of following hard after their God, we need to ensure they know we believe they were called to the task ahead. We need to speak words of courage over them, charging them with the task of carrying the gospel of Christ into the next generation, which needs Him desperately. And with that charge, we must give them our promise to stay engaged.

Strengthen

This is the work of training our little ones. Ruth Bell Graham said, "A true mother is not merely a provider, housekeeper, comforter, or companion. A true mother is primarily and essentially a trainer."[2] When we work to build muscles, an element of pain is involved in the strengthening process. We can expect no less from the process of developing wholehearted Christ followers. The keys are consistency, faithfulness, modeling, and prayer. I often cast myself upon the knowledge that the Father desires my children to follow Him faithfully even more than I do and that He will be the one to accomplish it. His Word will play a pivotal role. "All Scripture is breathed out by God and profitable for teaching, for reproof, for correction, and for training in righteousness, that the man of God may be complete, equipped for every good work" (2 Timothy 3:16-17).

Encourage

The journey ahead for our children will be filled with twists and turns, highs and lows. One day we'll be the ones whose voices fade and who lovingly draw the route ahead for our children to follow. If we equip them well and walk faithfully with the Lord, our final charge will find our children leaning in to hear words they know so well. They will ache with familiarity and love. We need to have handed them courage and spoken words of belief over them. I pray that, as our light dims and theirs blazes brightly, we will rest in the knowledge that they fight from a place of victory, and that as far as it depends on us we will have trained them well.

May it be so.

Here's to the sweaty training scenes, the ones where the preparation and transformation begin. This is no Disney movie. This is your leg of the race. Let's go.

Lord,

I commit my family to You and ask You to help me equip them for the path ahead. I praise and thank You that You have said You will never leave or forsake them. I say with confidence, "The Lord is my helper; I will not fear," as it says in Hebrews 13:6. Thank You, Father, that You are willing to help me raise my children and that You are deeply invested in the process. Help me to recognize areas where my children must be equipped and to do this work faithfully for Your glory. In Jesus's name, amen.

Part Three

The Noble Work

Character is built in a thousand small moments. The well-trained hero is shaped by the hand of someone equally as invested in the outcome as their protégé. We live and train for the glory of God. We are never alone in this journey, and fortunately for us, our Father's commitment and involvement in our process is unwavering.

11

Teach Them to Know and Obey Their God

*When obedience to God contradicts what I think will
give me pleasure, let me ask myself if I love Him.*
—Elisabeth Elliot

It's the stuff of parents' nightmares, or at the very least the stuff of my nightmares. Jerusalem had fallen. God had told His people through the prophets that they would be disciplined for their unfaithfulness to Him, and the time of chastisement was well upon them. Second Kings 24:10-17 describes the capture of the beautiful city in language that's hard to fathom. Nebuchadnezzar, king of Babylon, rides into Jerusalem and carries it away—ten thousand captives, all the nobility, all the craftsmen, all the men of valor, leaving only the poorest people of the land, who probably wouldn't have survived the trip to Babylon. The temple was decimated and looted, the walls were broken down, and families were killed or torn apart and carried away.

It would be tempting to believe that everyone was unfaithful to the Lord in the years prior to the Babylonian captivity of God's chosen people. But at least a remnant of Judah was teaching their children to know and obey Yahweh, the God of Israel. How do we know?

Because Daniel was among them, and as we read his story in Scripture and consider all he endured and how he thrived, I hope we see with X-ray eyes the parents who raised this hero of the faith.

Daniel was a young teenager when he was carried off to Babylon. Daniel 1 tells us,

> The king commanded Ashpenaz, his chief eunuch, to bring some of the people of Israel, both of the royal family and of the nobility, youths without blemish, of good appearance and skillful in all wisdom, endowed with knowledge, understanding learning, and competent to stand in the king's palace, and to teach them the literature and language of the Chaldeans (Daniel 1:3-4).

I told you, it's the stuff of nightmares. Most scholars believe Daniel and his royal buddies were 14 years old when they were taken.[1] I have a 13-year-old, and I don't think I could lift my head if he were carried off anywhere. I wonder right now how my Brendan would fare. Have I trained him well?

The Babylonians' plan was indoctrination of the cream of the Hebrew crop. Bring them in scared to death and strip away their identities as Hebrew youths, beginning with their names. Daniel, which means "God's judge," was changed to Belteshazzar, meaning "Bel's prince"—Bel being the chief of the Babylonian gods. Daniel's three friends, Hananiah, Mishael, and Azariah—meaning "Jehovah's gift," "the incomparableness of God," and "Jehovah our help"—received the new names Shadrach, Meshach, and Abednego. One commentator has said,

> When the court of Babylon wished to blot out from these Hebrew youths the memory of their fathers and the worship of the God of Israel, the very first thing was the changing of their names to correspond with the object

desired. But the expedient in this case did not succeed. Babylon began too late with these youths. Their names were changed, but their principles did not yield to the enchantment. Early instructions are not so easily obliterated. The impressions of childhoods are always the most lasting. They engrave themselves upon the formation of the man; they constitute the mould of one's being. They may be weakened and overlaid, but not extinguished. They are like words spoken in a whispering-gallery, which may not be heard near where they are uttered, but are produced in far-distant years and go echoing along the remotest paths of life... These youths had been brought up in the knowledge and worship of the true God, and had been taught His word and law; and their early teachings abode with them and remained proof against all the subtle seductions and expedients of a heathen court... Tyrants might change their names but their hearts remained loyal to the God of their fathers.[2]

I pray that, when it comes to our children, the Enemy might look at them and conclude, "We began too late. These kids already know their God." May our teachings echo down their heart chambers decades from now, reminding them of the truths we sow into them today.

What was sown into Daniel and his posse that allowed them to stand in enemy territory and become great heroes of the faith? I am certain of this: underneath the story of Daniel is a virtual carbon copy of what he held to be true about his God. I challenge you to read the book of Daniel with your kids, asking this question with every paragraph: What did Daniel know about God?

Daniel made some pivotal decisions in some of the first moments of his captivity that would determine the direction of his career and path. Upon arrival at the palace, the king gave the boys the richest foods, wines, and delicacies of his table. "But Daniel resolved that he would not defile himself with the king's food, or with the wine that he drank" (Daniel 1:8). In this instant, Daniel revealed the convictions he held at his core.

- An ultimate authority existed and King Nebuchadnezzar was not it. Although Daniel was in captivity to a foreign king and his life was in his hands, Daniel believed God was to be obeyed, come what may.
- His God was more powerful than this human king and was to be feared more than the human giving orders. If there is a place to start training our children, it must be this: there is a God and He has authority and power.
- The measure of obedience to God would come in his decision to avoid the rich foods of the king's table. They would not have been prepared the way God had prescribed and would have included food God had forbidden. Note how this first test is so similar to Eve's first test. It will never be a waste to remind our children that we can be enslaved by our appetites and cravings.
- Obedience to God is worth the risk. It may have seemed safer to eat the food placed in front of him, but through his actions Daniel demonstrated a fear of God greater than the fear of man. In kind, our focus must also circle back to teaching our children that the only remedy for fear itself is fear in the One who has all authority.

Daniel's proposal to the eunuch in charge of his care was simple. "Test your servants for ten days; let us be given vegetables to eat and water to drink. Then let our appearance and the appearance of the youths who eat the king's food be observed by you, and deal with your servants according to what you see" (Daniel 1:12-13).

The story becomes even more exciting than a boy asking to eat only vegetables and drink only water, though the thought is foreign to me as a farmer's wife. My teenage boy would be more apt to ask God to make a way through Mountain Dew and a pile of Cool Ranch Doritos.

> To these four young men God gave knowledge and understanding of all kinds of literature and learning. And Daniel could understand visions and dreams of all kinds. At the end of the time set by the king to bring them into his service, the chief official presented them to Nebuchadnezzar. The king talked with them, and he found none equal to Daniel, Hananiah, Mishael and Azariah; so they entered the king's service. In every matter of wisdom and understanding about which the king questioned them, he found them ten times better than all the magicians and enchanters in his whole kingdom (Daniel 1:17-20 NIV).

Ten times better. That is often my prayer for my teenager. *Somehow, Father, for Your glory, would You endow my son with such wisdom and understanding that people would seek his insight and guidance?*

A mere flip of the page in our Bibles finds Daniel in desperate need of the wisdom the Lord has given when the king threatens to kill all the wise men. Daniel responds to this new threat with the following words:

> Praise be to the name of God for ever and ever; wisdom and power are his. He changes times and seasons; he deposes kings and raises up others. He gives wisdom to the wise and knowledge to the discerning. He reveals deep and hidden things; he knows what lies in darkness, and light dwells with him. I thank and praise you, God of my ancestors (Daniel 2:20-23 NIV).

What does this reveal about the God Daniel knows? That His

name is powerful, that to Him belong power, wisdom, and might. That God changes the times and the seasons and the rulers of this world. That He is wise, sovereign, omniscient, outside of time, and worthy of Daniel's thanks and praise.

This is the beginning of what we can learn about what Daniel knew and believed about his God. The stories of the courage of Daniel and his crew become more and more encouraging and powerful.

Raising Theologians

A few years back the Christian Education Committee at my church, of which I am a part, made the decision to evaluate our children's curriculum. What we found was a complete deficiency in our program to teach our kids to think big thoughts about their God. The lessons told Bible stories but stopped short of offering the children a perspective of God as more than a flat character in a book. We were teaching kids the stories but failing to help them see that God is the center and primary character of the Bible, and that studying Scripture helps us to know Him and should lead us to worship. The entire committee felt dismayed. As we contemplated the best use of the hour we'd be given, we unanimously concluded that teaching our children to know the big God described in the Word should be at the top of the list. As we searched for curricula, we realized the material we chose and its scope and sequence were important, but that children will master what they are learning as they are discipled by their parents. Parents are the key factor for raising kids to know and obey their God.

My pastor preached an entire Sunday morning sermon on the development of our new philosophy and explained, "We are hoping to raise a church full of little theologians."

Our oldest huffed audibly in reply. He's as transparent as his mother, I'm afraid. When we got home Mike and I followed up on the huff and pout we heard from our son. "But I don't want to be a theologian! Theology is boring!" Mike and I asked him what theology meant, and he really had no answer.

Most of us have the very same thought process. Theology sounds boring. To the contrary, however, the study of God—or theology—is fascinating, and it's the parents' job to help God capture the hearts of their children. We can do this in three ways:

Model

First, we model the love and fascination for God we wish to see in our children. Do you find your heart captured by Him? For some of us, we love Him the most after a radiant sunrise, in the changing of the leaves, or when observing the glittering stars. We must let this love roll off our tongues. "God, what a delightful sunrise!" I often say as we drive to school. Mike models a fascination with plants and trees and points out the intricacies God has designed in the world around us. It can be as simple as a reminder that life itself is a surprising gift from the Lord, or by verbally relishing the power of His Word. As Deuteronomy 8:6-9 reminds us, all of life is relevant as we raise our children—walks along the road, when they lie down, as you sit together at home. All of life is relevant in training our children to walk with, know, and obey their God—not only moments in church, or even when we have our Bibles open on our laps, but in *all* of life.

Teach

Second, teach them the names of God and the stories that go with them. God has hundreds of names, and they are all useful in helping us know Him and the way He desires to work in the world around us. Tremendous resources are available to help us laymen parents who don't know the biblical languages of Hebrew and Greek crack open the nuances of the Word. Because when God reveals Himself as our creator, sovereign, protector, shield, defense, and our hope, that is only the beginning. He calls Himself full of wonders, the beginning of wisdom, the healer, our Savior, and our friend. We come to know Him as the God of angel armies, the beginning and the end, and yet our helper, comforter, and Father.

Honestly, knowing these things about Him is the reason we can trust Him enough to obey, because He tells us He is unchanging and true as well. This revelation of Himself to us through His Word is knowable. It requires little to guide young children into a high view of God. It begins with songs like, "My God is so big, so strong and so mighty/There's nothing my God cannot do." I hope you can hear the tune in your head. In the end this will become a great strength for your child because, "Those who know your name put their trust in you, for you, O Lord, have not forsaken those who seek you (Psalm 9:10).

Remind

Third, the lessons gain momentum as we lovingly remind our children it is God who ultimately deserves their obedience. Parents are merely vessels given the distinct privilege to love and train them to walk with their God. As faithful stewards of our "little theologians," let's lovingly remind them of the root issues in acts of disobedience and why they are an affront to the God to whom they belong. God meets rebellion with discipline. The author of Hebrews sums it up this way, beginning with referencing Proverbs 3:11-12:

> Have you completely forgotten this word of encouragement that addresses you as a father addresses his son? It says, "My son, do not make light of the Lord's discipline, and do not lose heart when he rebukes you, because the Lord disciplines the one he loves, and he chastens everyone he accepts as his son." Endure hardship as discipline; God is treating you as his children. For what children are not disciplined by their father? If you are not disciplined—and everyone undergoes discipline—then you are not legitimate, not true sons and daughters at all. Moreover, we have all had human fathers who disciplined us and we respected them for it. How much more should we submit to the Father of spirits and live! They disciplined us

for a little while as they thought best; but God disciplines us for our good, in order that we may share in his holiness. No discipline seems pleasant at the time, but painful. Later on, however, it produces a harvest of righteousness and peace for those who have been trained by it (Hebrews 12:5-11 NIV).

I'd do just about anything to raise up my children to experience a harvest of righteousness and peace. You too?

A Hero in the Family

Before heroes take defining leaps, their characters are built in thousands of small moments. Before Daniel stood before the king, he was raised by parents who taught him to honor and serve the Lord. Before they taught him to read, they taught him to talk and to pray. He learned the laws of his God and that no matter the situation, his God could be trusted. Before Mary became the mother of Jesus, she was a small girl who cried when she skinned her knees and who surely asked a thousand "why" questions. Before she praised God for allowing her to become the mother of the Savior, her parents taught her the truths she would pray. How do I know? Because heroes are grown, taught, admonished, and led into moments when their faith finds wings.

My mother-in-law, Karen, was raised in rural West Michigan on a fruit farm. She gave her heart to Christ at a little bitty age and remembers singing songs to the Lord while carefree on the swing in her front yard. She doesn't remember much about life before Jesus. Grandma often reminds me of the time when Karen walked into her mom's living room and seemed upset. Grandma switched off the vacuum and turned to find out why the tiny girl was out of sorts. "Mom, I can't decide if I want to be a missionary or a nurse." Grandma wisely advised her it was possible to be both, and Karen, seemingly satisfied with that answer, went back to playing. Looking back, it seems this was a prophetic moment. Karen would indeed have the chance to become both.

Karen met Dave at a youth group event, and the two fell in love. The downside was that Dave was leaving for college and would be attending Moody Bible Institute's Missionary Aviation program. Dave also loved the Lord, and he wanted to use his gifts to serve Him on the mission field as a pilot. As the two sought leading, their mutual love for Christ and heart for missions combined. Soon they found themselves married with two adorable kids (I'm married to the oldest) and serving with Mission Aviation Fellowship (MAF) in the Indonesian jungle.

Missionary pilots fly into areas that are difficult or impossible to reach by car and may take days or even weeks to access by hiking trails. They transport missionaries, doctors, and supplies, and fly in relief supplies during times of disaster and hardship. They really are heroes. Their schedules and routes depend on weather, and the airstrips where they land are often unpaved and treacherous.

Dave loved being a pilot and Karen loved being a pilot's wife. They fell in love with their teammates and the Danii people of Indonesia.

One morning in 1985, Dave kissed his wife good-bye and walked out the door for a routine trip. As Karen laid in bed, she thought she heard a plane engine shut off, but paid no real attention. She walked into the kitchen, switched on the flight-following radio as usual, and began her morning. Then she heard one of the men on the radio ask if the other could see "it." Soon there was a knock at the door and another pilot's wife entered her home.

"Karen, there's been an accident."

"Who?"

"Dave."

"Which Dave?"

"Yours."

Karen has told me she did the only thing she knew to do. She gathered her youngest and said, "We need to pray. Daddy may have gone to be with Jesus." In the days that followed, Karen knew the presence and hand of her God. She looks back at that painful time and sees how the God she had grown to love and know led her and the kids all the way. She sees the miracles that happened, the people who cared and came. In the days and months that followed, her Dave would fight for his life, their family would move back to the States, and Karen would learn her high school sweetheart would never be the same. Dave's hip was crushed, leaving him unable to walk without assistance, and he had a severe head injury that would never go away. Today Dave recognizes his family and a few close friends and has a joyful spirit and love for the Lord, but a mind that has virtually no short-term memory and a long-term memory with gaping holes. He is childlike in so many ways, and with that crash their married life as they had known it was forever changed.

We have two heroes here—Dave, who in many ways lost his life, and his wife, Karen, who has lovingly been his caretaker for over 30 years. If you were to ask her today how she has managed, she will direct you to the God who has loved and sustained her and her boys all these years. She would tell you about getting through nursing school with a husband who needed constant attention and two little boys who needed her like crazy. She will tell you that the key to it all was holding on to the Lord. In an age of nearly disposable marriages, her commitment to the Lord has superseded her desire for the companionship of another man, and that alone moves others to ask about the God she serves. She's a hero of the faith.

> Blessed is the man who trusts in the LORD, whose trust is the LORD. He is like a tree planted by water, that sends out its roots by the stream, and does not fear when heat comes, for its leaves remain green, and is not anxious in the year of drought, for it does not cease to bear fruit (Jeremiah 17:7-8).

Lord,

We have no greater prayer than that our children will learn to know You. Knowing who You are in Your might, power, and goodness is just the beginning. I ask that You will be the greatest fascination of their lives and that from that knowledge will flow worship, humility, courage, and trust. I pray that in every way my children will find You worthy of their obedience and devotion. I trust, Father, that whatever may come, You will prepare my children for it, enabling them to walk in the security and assuredness of Your presence. You are good, and I trust You to yield fruit in my children. In Jesus's name, amen.

12

Teach Them About the Value of the Word of God

Imagine if we started raising generations of children who stood uncompromisingly on the Word of God, knew how to defend the Christian faith, could answer the skeptical questions of this age, and had a fervor to share the gospel from the authority of God's Word with whomever they met! This could change the world.

—KEN HAM

"I'd give money to help smuggle Bibles into Iran."

The words caught me off guard. I was sitting in my living room surrounded by the girls from our high school youth group. They came every other Sunday night to have Bible study and laugh together. Each week I'd prepare for them by looking around the grocery store for junk food that was economical and might feed 30 hungry teenage girls. Pizza rolls and Twizzlers are always a hit, or warm brownies. Chocolate seems like a common denominator among women of all ages.

Most nights I'd ask a get-to-know-you question, and the results were always telling. One night I asked them where they'd go shopping if I gave them a store gift card. Most would spend their money in a clothing store or on iTunes. But on this night the question was, "If I gave you a $1000 to give away to a nonprofit, a church, or a cause close to your heart, who would you give the money to?" The answers were precious. The girls said they would share their money with places such as an orphan care program, with missionaries they loved, or with inner city care programs. All the answers were precious in their own right, but the answer that stunned me was the one that involved the most risk.

"I'd give money to help smuggle Bibles into Iran."

The answer had come from my son, who was only seven at the time. My family would always begin those Bible study nights with us laughing and snuggling with the girls. From time to time they would sit in on the fun-sharing question, and sometimes if they had an answer they would give it. I was relatively amazed by two things. The first was that he knew where Iran was and that Bible smuggling was necessary. The second was that he knew that to risk one's life for others to have access to the Word of God was worth it.

Right now, heroes are laying down their lives so others can read the life-changing Word of God. Our friends Jared and Melanie serve with an organization in the jungle of Papua, Indonesia. They are working with an indigenous tribe of people who have never been reached with the gospel. Their language has still never been written down. Jared and Melanie and their three kids have faced terrible sickness already, with little or at least slow access to medical care, because they believe God deeply enough to be there. They want His Word in the hands of others.

> Our children should not starve for hearing the Word of God when we have the Bread of the Word on our nightstands.

In my home right now, I probably have 20 copies of the Word of God, a disproportionately high number of Bibles. But my guess is that if you have the luxury of holding this book in your hands, you also own multiple copies of the Word. I have an app on my phone that just told me it has 48 English versions on it. Forty-eight different versions of the Word in English. I know they aren't all equal, and I don't necessarily recommend you study out of all of them, but you could come to know Jesus if you read any of them. Yet we have people throughout the world who cannot access the Sword of the Spirit, the Word of God.

Friends, our children are not among those, yet they are being raised in one of the most biblically illiterate generations in recent history. Amos 8:11 tells us, "'Behold, the days are coming.' declares the Lord God, 'when I will send a famine on the land—not a famine of bread, nor a thirst for water, but of hearing the words of the Lord.'" Our children should not starve for hearing the Word of God when we have the Bread of the Word on our nightstands.

48 from 1

William Tyndale was a master of languages. By the time he was 21, he could speak seven languages and had mastery of both Greek and Hebrew. By the time he was 30, William burned with a God-given passion to translate the Bible from its original languages into English, which had never been done. At that time, in the early 1500s, the Word of God was accessible only to priests who were trained to read Greek and Hebrew.

When William shared his vision with the bishop of London, he was "strongly opposed" by the English church, which did not believe lay people could rightly handle the Word and should be prevented from having access to it.[1] But Tyndale replied, "If God spare my life, ere many years, I will cause a boy that driveth the plough to know more of the Scripture than thou dost."[2] While Martin Luther's German translation was making waves throughout Europe, William set himself to the task of translating the Scriptures.

This God-given passion and the backlash that resulted drove William from his home in England to Germany. In 1525, two years after he began, the first New Testament translation into English was finished. Within a short time, England was flooded with 15,000 copies of the English New Testament.

While working on the Old Testament translation, William Tyndale was betrayed by a man he thought was a friend to the gospel. In May of 1535, he was arrested on charges of heresy, stripped of his title as priest, and on October 6, 1536, he was strangled and then burned at the stake in Brussels. English historian John Foxe said he cried out, "Lord, open the King of England's eyes!"[3]

The story of William Tyndale's sacrifice to translate the Word of God into English should not be kept from our children, who are now able to hold a copy of the Scripture in their hands. The apostle Paul tells us, "All Scripture is God-breathed and is useful for teaching, rebuking, correcting and training in righteousness, so that the servant of God may be thoroughly equipped for every good work" (2 Timothy 3:16-17 NIV). Nothing else makes the claim to thoroughly equip our children for the road ahead like Scripture does. It is not supplemental material to tuck onto the end of our days with them, but rather the framework from which to build their spiritual lives.

Is that how you view Scripture, as the training tool you can't be without?

Completely Convinced

What would make a woman get up morning after morning, day after day, and pore over a copy of an archaic book when she could be sleeping? Why not stay in bed after waiting up for her teenager to come home or being up at night with a sick child? What motivates someone to devote free time to Scripture memory or do devotions with her children? Only a mother who is completely convinced in the life-changing and life-giving benefits of the Word of God sacrifices precious hours of sleep or free time. It strikes me that Tyndale and others throughout history willingly gave up their lives so we can read Scripture. In light of their sacrifice, what would keep me from a half hour with God's Word in the morning?

The questions for you today, dear one, are these: Are you completely convinced that the Bible holds the answers your family needs? Are you fascinated by it, do you savor it, do you make it relevant, do you bathe your children in it? Do you make connections between what you read and what your family is experiencing? Remember, your children will learn to love and value the Word of God by watching you drink it in and experience its benefits first.

Psalm 119 is chock-full of reasons to devote our time and attention to getting the Word into us and our children. Tonight, as I read the Word with eyes trained on the value added to our lives from a study and devotion to the Word, I was struck afresh how necessary it is in the life of a believer. Scripture

- teaches us about the character of God (verse 7)
- teaches us the promises He has made to us (verse 116)
- assures us of His faithfulness (verse 90)
- comforts us (verse 76)
- shows us God's way (verse 3)
- gives us knowledge and teaches good judgment (verse 66)
- gives us understanding and teaches us to value truth (verse 104)
- keeps us from sin (verse 11)
- teaches us about purity (verse 9)
- strengthens us (verse 28)
- gives us life (verse 37)
- promises blessing (verse 1)

As though those reasons are not enough, the Word is so completely dynamic. It's not stagnant and fixed in time, unlike any other book we can hold in our hands. "The word of God is *living* and *active*, sharper than any two-edged sword, piercing to the division of soul and of spirit, of joints and of marrow, and discerning the thoughts and intentions of the heart" (Hebrews 4:12, emphasis added). This is great news for all of us because, although the Word is changeless, it remains relevant to our generation and the one we raise.

Love Wisdom

If a word is missing from our kids' vocabularies it might be the word *wisdom*. Wisdom is scarcely seen in the world today, difficult to recognize, and highly devalued. Its opposite—folly—seems to be getting all the airtime. Perhaps we're sliding away from wisdom because of the decrease in our attention spans. As a friend of mine recently pointed out, it's hard to find a wise YouTube video. And the TV shows that entertain us rarely point us in the way of righteousness, and often make lines to what should be absolute seem blurry.

One of my kids' favorite commercials has two wives sitting across the pool from their husbands, talking about where to find the closest emergency room. They're looking at the hospital ratings on an app on their smartphones while their husbands engage in stupidity that will land both of them in the hospital. The pole vaulting onto the concrete instead of into the swimming pool is just another hilarious example of why this generation celebrates folly over wisdom. Folly is fun for a season, while wisdom constantly applies experience and right judgment. I thought this might just apply to this twenty-first-century era, but King Solomon puts a face on wisdom for us and tells us about her quest to find someone who will listen.

> Wisdom cries aloud in the street, in the markets she raises her voice; at the head of the noisy streets she cries out; at the entrance of the city gates she speaks: "How long, O simple ones, will you love being simple? How long will scoffers delight in their scoffing and fools hate knowledge? If you turn at my reproof, behold, I will pour out my spirit to you; I will make my words known to you" (Proverbs 1:20-23).

But Solomon's lady wisdom finds no takers, and when disaster strikes, those who failed to listen to wisdom are devastated. Experience tells us this is true. We see this happening in every political system. People fail to apply wisdom and fall flat on their faces.

Then they will call upon me, but I will not answer; they will seek me diligently but will not find me. Because they hated knowledge and did not choose the fear of the LORD, would have none of my counsel and despised all my reproof, therefore they shall eat the fruit of their way, and have their fill of their own devices. For the simple are killed by their turning away, and the complacency of fools destroys them; but whoever listens to me will dwell secure and will be at ease, without dread of disaster (Proverbs 1:28-33).

> God's Word tucked into our minds and hearts provides a compass for navigating when the world warps and sways.

Not only do our kids need to take the time to grow in wisdom, but like Solomon we must take the time to teach them. At my house, I've found it is a constant battle to clear room in our schedules for time in the Word together. We have lunches to pack, meals to make, and then clean up, and we must drive to school or be up early enough to catch the bus on time. I'm just as guilty as the next person for allowing my follow-through to wane or for allowing parenthood to become so complicated a job that I struggle to get it done at all. But when we consider the dire consequences of not teaching our children to learn to develop wisdom and then listen when it calls, I'm pretty sure we'll find the time. When we come to grips with the truth that Scripture is not a behavior modification plan, but the road map to life abundant, we'll begin to take great pleasure in engaging our children with it.

Bible memorization is a key to teaching our children to discern wisdom from folly and to equip them to live in a culture that has lost its bearings. The psalmist says, "I have stored up your word in my heart, that I might not sin against you" (Psalm 119:11). God's Word tucked into our minds and hearts provides a compass for navigating when the world warps and sways. Knowing the Word of God gives our children an internal script that lasts a lifetime. Their young minds have been designed to retain. Trust me, it will prove much easier for them to memorize long passages than it will be for you. Make it fun, sing the Word, develop challenges, bribe them if you must, but get the Word in. "Solid food is for the mature, who by constant use have trained themselves to distinguish good from evil" (Hebrews 5:14 NIV). Knowing good from evil is truly a life-giving matter.

Change a Heart, Change a Nation

The nation of Israel was in shambles. King Solomon had built a majestic temple in Jerusalem to honor the God of Israel, the God of his father, David. But though the glory of the Lord filled the temple, Solomon's heart was led astray.

> He had 700 wives, who were princesses, and 300 concubines. And his wives turned away his heart. For when Solomon was old his wives turned away his heart after other gods, and his heart was not wholly true to the Lord his God...Then Solomon built a high place for Chemosh the abomination of Moab, and for Molech the abomination of the Ammonites, on the mountain east of Jerusalem. And so he did for all his foreign wives, who made offerings and sacrificed to their gods (1 Kings 11:3-4,7-8).

On a hill in view of the temple, the king built shrines to the gods of his wives. It's shocking. It's easy to build a base of faith in our families and then chase after lesser things. Under Solomon's leadership, the nation of Israel was led astray. The sin he committed would not be overlooked by God, and God ripped the nation of Israel in two, giving ten tribes to Solomon's servant, Jeroboam. These ten tribes would be called Israel, or the northern kingdom. Jeroboam would be their first king and he would make his residence in the town of Shechem. That was only the start of the division of the kingdoms, and two kingdoms meant everything would need to be reframed.

Jeroboam was rightfully afraid that if his people returned to Jerusalem to worship at the temple, their hearts would return to the king of Judah. He began reframing worship for his people by having two calves fashioned out of gold and placed in two different cities, Bethel and Dan. I hope the irony of Jeroboam fashioning gold calves and the Israelites fashioning golden calves with Aaron while Moses was up on the mountain isn't lost on you. Shouldn't the cow thing have at least sort of seemed familiar in their minds? Regardless, the situation quickly became tragic.

A man of God came from Judah, the southern kingdom, to Bethel, where Jeroboam was standing and making offerings by the calf. He cried out, "'O altar, altar, thus says the LORD: "Behold, a son shall be born to the house of David, Josiah by name, and he shall sacrifice on you the priests of the high places who make offerings on you, and human bones shall be burned on you"'" (1 Kings 13:2). To make a long story shorter, over the next 210 years 19 kings would reign over Israel and not one of them would be godly. In 722 BC, the capital city of Samaria would fall to the Assyrians and the tribes of Israel would be taken.

Meanwhile, the tribes of Judah and Benjamin would form the southern kingdom and be ruled by Solomon's son Rehoboam. Only a promise God made to King David, and certainly not the righteousness of the people nor the heart of the king, kept the Lord from obliterating the entire race.

> For David's sake the LORD his God gave him a lamp in Jerusalem, setting up his son after him, and establishing Jerusalem, because David did what was right in the eyes of the LORD and did not turn aside from anything that he commanded him all the days of his life, except in the matter of Uriah the Hittite [Bathsheba's husband] (1 Kings 15:4-5).

The temple in Jerusalem would continue to be the center of

worship for the tribes now known as Judah. But worship over the next 200 years would never look the same. A cycle of kings would begin, some spending their reign desecrating and dishonoring the God of Judah and others doing their best to rebuild and renew the faith of their people. This almost reads like a current history textbook, doesn't it?

The darkest days for the tribe of Judah and the city of Jerusalem were undoubtedly during the reign of Manasseh. False worship had existed until this point, but Manasseh took it to an entirely different stratosphere. He built altars and high places for the worship of Baal and Asherah. He built altars in the temple of the Lord and altars in the courts of the temple. He burned his son as an offering to a false god, and 2 Kings 21:16 tells us, "Manasseh shed very much innocent blood, till he had filled Jerusalem from one end to another, besides the sin that he made Judah to sin so that they did what was evil in the sight of the LORD." Manasseh ransacked the temple of God Most High, corrupted all worship there, and filled the land with evil that would make even our modern minds whirl.

His 55-year reign in Jerusalem undoubtedly made the streets seem like Gotham City, nowhere resembling Jerusalem, the bright and beautiful city of God. His son Amon would briefly reign for two evil years until he was assassinated by his servants, and those people made Amon's eight-year-old son king. The boy's name was Josiah.

Something was different about Josiah from the start, because who in their right mind would assassinate a king and put an eight-year-old on the throne? If people wanted the throne for themselves or for another, they surely could have taken it by force. But that was not the choice. Evil had flourished and been celebrated for 57 years. The temple was in shambles, idols were on every hilltop, and the images of child sacrifices still lingered in the people's minds. When we read about Josiah's first defining moment as king, he is a tender 26 years old, but already in the eighteenth year of his reign. In that year, something in Josiah stirred to repair the house of the Lord. During the restoration process, the high priest, named Hilkiah, finds the Book of the Law. Evidently it had been missing. How long? I wonder.

> Hilkiah the high priest said to Shaphan the secretary, "I have found the Book of the Law in the house of the LORD." And Hilkiah gave the book to Shaphan, and he read it... Then Shaphan the secretary told the king, "Hilkiah the priest has given me a book." And Shaphan read it before the king. When the king heard the words of the Book of the Law, he tore his clothes" (2 Kings 22:8,10-11).

The grief that overtook King Josiah, and probably the fear of God as well, was immediate, demonstrative, and strong. As the boy king looked at his nation, he saw the gravity of the situation. The things he had been read in no way resembled the culture of his kingdom. They were all law breakers before the Lord. "Great is the wrath of the LORD that is kindled against us, because our fathers have not obeyed the words of this book, to do according to all that is written concerning us" (2 Kings 22:13).

Josiah quickly sends Hilkiah the high priest to inquire of the Lord. Ironically, this priest has no special channel to God and has been priest without a manual all these years. Instead of heading to the temple of God, or to the prophets Jeremiah and Zephaniah, who were alive and well, they head to a prophetess who's married to the royal keeper of the wardrobe. (You can't make this stuff up, you guys.) The message that comes back from the prophetess is bleak. Judah will be struck by disaster just as Josiah suspected, but not on his watch.

> This is what the LORD, the God of Israel, says concerning the words you heard: Because your heart was responsive and you humbled yourself before the LORD when you heard what I have spoken against this place and its people—that they would become a curse and be laid waste—and because you tore your robes and wept in my presence,

I also have heard you, declares the LORD. Therefore I will gather you to your ancestors, and you will be buried in peace. Your eyes will not see all the disaster I am going to bring on this place (2 Kings 22:18-20 NIV).

The story of Josiah and the actions he takes next are unbelievably important. So much is here about the value of the Word of God in the life of believers, and we must teach our kids about the power that's released as we read and obey the Word.

Important Lesson #1—God's Word Still Has Powerful Effect in Those Who Hear It

Romans 10:17 (NIV)—"Consequently, faith comes from hearing the message, and the message is heard through the word about Christ."

We do not live in an environment where the Word of God is missing. We have instead reached a time when it's unusual to hear it spoken. We may even attend churches where the messages sound like godliness but miss the meat of the Word of God. We can't settle in this area. Our children must hear the Word of the Lord. They are still the only words that promise they will not return without effect (Isaiah 55:11). Paul makes this perfectly clear when he tells his protégé Timothy, "Until I come, devote yourself to the public reading of Scripture, to preaching and to teaching" (1 Timothy 4:13 NIV).

Moms, there is incredible power in washing our children with the Word of God and giving them the opportunity to engage with its mind-renewing power. After all, "all Scripture is God-breathed and is useful for teaching, rebuking, correcting and training in righteousness, so that the servant of God may be thoroughly equipped for every good work" (2 Timothy 3:16-17 NIV).

Important Lesson #2—Obedience to God's Word Produces Life Change

We can no longer merely survey the devastation of the culture around us. We must grab hold of the Word and obey. When Josiah heard the words of the Lord, the clean sweep began inside him. He wept, he tore his clothes, and he sent intercessors to seek God. When our children encounter the Word of the Lord, it must produce life change inside them as well, or we risk seeing them develop calloused hearts.

As we discipline, we need to make sure we hold Scripture as the standard and not our own expectations. That means our children obey us not because we are bigger than they are and in charge, but because the Lord has told them to honor us that it may go well with them (Ephesians 6:2-3). We want them to learn not to whine, act selfishly, steal, sleep around, or snark at the authorities in their lives because God said not to, not because we have tried to produce children who are easier to handle or can be successful in the world. We're looking for transformed and renewed minds.

"You were taught, with regard to your former way of life, to put off your old self, which is being corrupted by its deceitful desires; to be made new in the attitude of your minds; and to put on the new self, created to be like God in true righteousness and holiness" (Ephesians 4:22-24 NIV).

Important Lesson #3–God's Word Still Transforms Nations

King Josiah heard the words of the Lord and went to the temple calling all the people—and I do mean all—to him. He personally read the words of the Book of the Law to them and then personally renewed the covenant with the Lord.

> The king stood by the pillar and made a covenant before the LORD, to walk after the LORD and to keep his commandments and his testimonies and his statutes with all his heart and all his soul, to perform the words of this covenant that were written in this book. And all the people joined in the covenant (2 Kings 23:3).

Heroes of the faith lead the way in repentance and resolve to obey God with heart and soul. Josiah and the people began to purge Judah of the idols. No two stones were left one on the other at the high places, the temple was cleaned, and anything that defiled his country in the eyes of his God was destroyed. The job was thorough, and within one year Judah had been completely purged of its idolatry. So great was Josiah's commitment to reclaim ground for the Lord that he journeyed to the old northern kingdom city of Israel, Bethel, and tore down the altars there, fulfilling a 300-year, name-specific prophecy. At the end of the year he ordered the celebration of Passover, and Scripture records there had never been a celebration as deep or thorough of that holiday as the one celebrated by King Josiah.

Josiah's story should fill us with incredible hope. No period of darkness is without hope, and no climate is so dark that God's light cannot permeate it. We must cling to God's Word and teach our kids diligently that it holds transformative power for them and this generation.

Father,
Your Word is life to us. Though it has remained unchanging with time, it continues to be completely relevant to our world today. Etch Your Word onto the hearts of my children and give them hearts eager to learn and obey. As they seek You in Your Word, will You meet with them and impart understanding and wisdom for living as Your children in their generation? May they savor that time with You and be diligent to hide it in their hearts. Use Your Word to correct them and encourage them today. I'm asking that they will hunger after truth and find the direction they need in Scripture. In the name of the living Word, Jesus, I pray, amen.

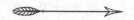

Teach Them to Pray

*Would you have your child called early into divine service
and separated from the world unto God? Would you have
him so situated that he will be called in childhood by the
Spirit of God? Put him under prayer influences…If more
children were born of praying mothers, brought up in direct
contact with "the house of prayer," and reared under prayer
environments, more children would hear the voice of God's
Spirit speaking to them, and would more quickly respond to
those divine calls to a religious life. Would we have praying
men in our churches? We must have praying mothers
to give them birth, praying homes to color their lives, and
praying surroundings to impress their minds and to lay the
foundations for praying lives. Praying Samuels come from
praying Hannahs. Praying priests come from "the house
of prayer." Praying leaders come from praying homes.*

—E. M. BOUNDS

I knelt before my son and laid my head down on the floor. He put his hand on my back and began to pray.

"Lord, use my mama. Give her the right words and help these women to hear from You." It was a commissioning prayer, and there was no doubt in my mind that the Lord leaned down to hear. It was a sacred moment for both of us. But we didn't start here, and just like everything that becomes instinctual, prayer was a skill that was cultivated and developed in my children.

Unfortunately, many parents feel inept in the area of prayer themselves and feel ill-equipped to teach their children. Whether we're skilled intercessors with children who already love to pray or newbies who aren't sure where to begin, we need to make sure we understand a few things in our hearts and then teach our families.

Just as vigilant praying mamas need to carve prayer routines into their lives, our children need to cultivate prayer habits and practice them. Charlotte Mason, a Christian education specialist, said, "As has been well said, 'Sow an act, reap a habit; sow a habit; reap a character; sow a character, reap a destiny.' And a great function of the educator is to secure that acts shall be so regularly, purposefully and methodically sown that the child shall reap the habits of the good life, in thinking and doing, with the minimum of conscious effort."[1]

What we are looking for, then, is grooves to be cut so deep in our family life that our children breathe prayer. When they are frightened, they pray, and when they are victorious, they pray. We want children who know the answer to every question is found in the Father and by seeking His will in their lives. Can this be a reality? Yes, I really believe so. I'm seeing it happen in my family, and I'm experiencing the deeply humbling and rich benefits of having children who really pray.

Prayer Habits

Natural places exist to begin teaching our children to pause and give thanks through prayer. Prayers of thanks before meals are a good place to start, and with toddlers it's good to teach them the habit of closing their eyes and bowing their heads out of reverence to the Father and to avoid distraction. I think it's important to give them the language to understand what they're doing and why it's so important. Praying with a two-year-old would often mean saying, "Brendan, it's time to thank our heavenly Father for this yummy food. It's so good to say thank you, isn't it? Can you bow your head like Mama and close your eyes while we talk to God? It helps us pay attention better, doesn't it? Good job, buddy." Then for the first year and a half you can invite them to listen while you pray, modeling simple prayers of thanksgiving, such as "Thank You, God, for this food. You take good care of us and we love You. Amen."

Of course, modeling also happens when you allow them to be present and included when your prayers are longer. As our children have grown, we've had them repeat prayers after us, fill in the blank with foods they are grateful for, and have expected them to be attentive. After a while we began asking them to bless the meal, allowing them to respectfully freestyle on their own. Now our mealtime prayers are usually lively and filled with sweet times of listening to their hearts.

Capitalizing on moments already in the day is a great way to begin to create a beautiful atmosphere of prayer. Other natural prayer breaks in the day are:

- Bedtime—Rehearse God's faithfulness that day and add prayers for special people they have encountered and people in their lives who need the Lord.
- When they are ill—Pray with them asking God to make their tummy feel better and the doctor to have wisdom.
- After times of discipline—Help them learn the process of repentance and asking for forgiveness.
- When they are happy—Have them thank God for a beautiful day. Thank Him for fun activities and new experiences.
- Emergency vehicles—Whenever you pass a fire truck, ambulance, or police car, use that time to pray together for the people involved in the accident or situation. Ask for the Father to give wisdom and peace and to use this life interruption to bring people to Him.

- Watching the news—Grab a map and locate the place that faces a prayer need and pray.
- When we don't know what to do—This is one of my favorite times to pray with my kids because it helps them understand that, although we don't have the answers, our God does!

My youngest, Ryan, often talks to me about his prayer life, which appears to be rowdy after he heads to bed. He's learning to rehearse the day and tell the Lord what's on his mind. He asks for what he needs and often asks for help falling asleep. Sometimes when he creeps down at night and tells me he can't sleep I'll ask him if he's talked to the Lord about it. Quite often the answer is already a big yes and he just needs one more cuddle. Or a glass of water. Or a cracker. Or one more hug. You know the drill.

> Home is the tapestry I weave day in and day out, and prayer in the loom upon which I place my thread.
> —Darlene Schacht

It Can Be (and Probably Should Be) Simple

A darling friend of my daughter's sat at our table for dinner. They had just come in from jumping on the trampoline and they both were pink-cheeked and a little sweaty. Piles of food sat on the table and I briefly said, "At our home, we thank God for the food He has given us before we eat. We'll do that really quickly and then we can dig in." Without any hint of hesitation or shame, her sweet eyes looked right back at me and said, "I don't know how."

My daughter piped right up and said, "That's okay. Praying is easy. It's just talking." Since she was on such a roll, I turned and asked Gabi to go ahead and lead us in prayer. "Thank You, Jesus, for this food and for this day. Thank You for the trampoline and that I could have a friend over today. Be with Angela and Mareto [the Compassion International kids we sponsor] and help their families to have enough today. In Jesus's name, amen." Then she said to her friend, "See, it's easy." And that was that.

I'm often surprised at how easy evangelistic praying with unbelievers can be. Our natural instinct is to skip a quick prayer when we have lunch with friends who don't believe. Not one time, however, have I been told no when I've asked if I could pray for our meal or pray on the spot for a need I knew someone had. To the contrary, many, many times these friends and acquaintances thank me for praying for them and have even gone so far as to say they were deeply touched.

> Keeping our prayers simple and straightforward isn't just a good idea for training our children; it's God's idea for right conversation.

The idea is not the impressiveness of the prayers we pray, but the great God we pray them to and His invitation to bring our needs. Jesus said, "When you pray, don't babble on and on as the Gentiles [people of other religions] do. They think their prayers are answered merely by repeating their words again and again" (Matthew 6:7 NLT). Keeping our prayers simple and straightforward isn't just a good idea for training our children; it's God's idea for right conversation.

The disciples were astounded by the ease with which Jesus prayed to the Father. When they heard Him pray it was different. There was an air of closeness and familiarity. Jesus told them, "When you pray, go into your room and shut the door and pray to your Father who is in secret...your Father knows what you need before you ask him. Pray then like this: 'Our Father in heaven, hallowed be your name'" (Matthew 6:6,8-9).

Titles are everything, and while we must teach our children that God deserves all honor and reverence ("hallowed be your name"), they are told to address Him with a term of endearment and familiarity—Father, or even Dad. This astounding ability to approach the God of the universe as His child is a blood-bought right that cost the Father His Son. Refusing to enter His presence often is like forfeiting winning a great prize and surrendering an honor that could be ours.

Four Steps of Prayer

I told you in the vigilant prayer chapter that learning to pray the four steps of prayer with Moms in Prayer International changed everything for me. It brought order to my thoughts and allowed me to move with a strategy through my prayer in a way that felt natural and structured. I began feeling successful in covering requests and specific areas that had been previously undeveloped. I understand that not everyone appreciates formulas, but these four steps feel like freedom to me rather than confinement. Each step builds on the next, and while they are powerful enough to revolutionize an adult's prayer life, they are simple enough for a small child to understand.

Step One: Praise

We begin with praising God for who He tells us He is and for what He tells us He's like. Scripture describes God with literally hundreds of different names and attributes. The interesting thing about starting here is that it builds our confidence in who God is. When I was younger, I found it difficult to express the greatness of God, to God. I knew He was big and I knew He saved me through Christ, but when I was told to praise Him, I got lost when I moved beyond the words *big*, *good*, and *strong*. This is where teaching our kids to praise Him using Scripture helps.

The Lord tells us He is our

- Comfort
- Hiding Place
- Firm Foundation
- Hope
- Peace

- Teacher
- Shelter
- Shield
- Refuge
- Hope

- Shepherd
- Friend
- Savior
- Helper

- Promise Keeper
- Creator
- Strong Defense

He describes Himself as

- Loving
- Close
- Forgiving
- Gracious
- Victorious
- Strong
- Faithful
- Compassionate
- Gentle

- Wise
- Jealous
- Sovereign
- Present
- Healing
- Nurturing
- Powerful
- Good

Our children must know Him as

- The Lord of Hosts
- The God Who Sees
- The Father of Prodigals
- The Lamb of God
- The Lion of Judah

- The Beginning and The End
- The Great I Am
- The Father
- The Suffering Servant
- The Spirit

Psalm 100 tells us to "enter his gates with thanksgiving and his courts with praise; give thanks to him and praise his name" (verse 4 NIV). Why start with praise? Because God needs to be reminded how great He is? No! We start with praise because He knows *we* need to be reminded how great He is. Praise helps activate within us all a sense of awe and reverence that will lead to humility. Praise honors God by giving Him the esteem due Him.

Teaching your children to pray with praise might begin by reading a passage of Scripture and choosing one of the attributes in the Word, or by saying, "We praise You God because You are _____!" My kids often yell words like *big, strong, caring, mighty,* and *good.* And then you could echo back an agreement and add on to the prayer. "Yes, God, we do praise You because You are good. We praise You that You are always good and that cannot change. Every choice You make is good."

I tend to linger here longer and longer now. Rehearsing the greatness of my God causes everything else to still before Him. My problems and my kids' problems become manageable and small in the hands of our loving Father. Praise builds me up, even more than it builds up our God.

Step Two: Confession

Confession never feels good at the start, but God's kindness to us leads us to repentance (Romans 2:4). It's as simple as saying, "God, I'm sorry that I _____," or "God, I shouldn't have _____." When my children and I practice confession together, sometimes I feel comfortable confessing my sin aloud and other times I know that should remain private between God and me.

Let's teach our kids to practice both public and private confession as well. When they're young, we can model confession for them and have them repeat after us as we model what repentant prayers look like. As they grow, however, it is also appropriate to encourage them to pray inside their hearts to their Father in heaven.

Remind them that this is the time to address specific sins—not the entire day's worth, but taking one at a time. As we teach them to do this on their own, we must remind them that we can confess in every

moment of the day, not only by truckload in the evening before bed.
Each sin has a corresponding consequence, and each one breaks fellowship with the Lord and with others. The great news, though, is
that they have all been covered by Christ's death on the cross and He
is eager to forgive.

If you teach your kids only one verse about confession, let it be this
one: "If we confess our sins, he is faithful and just to forgive us our sins
and to cleanse us from all unrighteousness" (1 John 1:9).

We have the privilege of going to God knowing our sins will be
forgiven. What a tremendous gift and relief to our children's minds
as they realize Jesus doesn't weigh each sin, trying to decide if He will
forgive. He has already decided to take the consequence for each one.
Hallelujah!

Step Three: Thanksgiving

If your family is anything like our family, this step of praying
together can be a blast. This is when we say thank you for all God has
done. Truth be told, this is the step that provides an instantaneous
attitude adjustment in all of us. Thanksgiving changes me. It releases
discontentment and embraces the gifts that have been given. Just like
confession, thanksgiving needs to be specific. This can be easily cultivated in our children as they identify large and small blessings they
are grateful for—shoes, their home, the dog, their church, or anything at all.

It seems so simple, so obvious, that we should give thanks. Isn't
that one of the first things we teach our children? Luke 17 records a
time when ten men's bodies, damaged because of leprosy, were healed
by Christ and only one man returned to express thanks. Jesus marvels
and says, "Were not ten cleansed? Where are the nine? Was no one
found to return and give praise to God?" (verses 17-18). In her incredible book *One Thousand Gifts,* Ann Voskamp explores the power of
living a life of thanksgiving, but first she deals with a heart issue that
cannot be left unchecked: ingratitude.

> The sin of ingratitude. Adam and Eve are, simply, painfully, ungrateful for what God gave. Isn't that the catalyst of all my sins? Our fall was, has always been, and always will be, that we aren't satisfied in God and what He gives. We hunger for something more, something other. Standing before that tree, laden with fruit withheld, we listen to Evil's murmur, 'In the day you eat from it your eyes will be opened' (Genesis 3:5 NASB). But in the beginning, our eyes were already open. Our sight was perfect. Our vision let us see a world spilling with goodness. Our eyes fell on nothing but the glory of God. We saw God as He truly is: good.[2]

Ann goes on to explain that when Adam and Eve ate the apple they believed would give them sight or open their eyes to good and evil, they instead received blindness. Blindness to the goodness of the Lord. Friends, this matter of giving thanks to the Father isn't just about a good prayer habit. It is truly life-changing. We need to teach our kids to fight discouragement, discontentment, and ingratitude, using the supernatural weapon of thanksgiving. Recognizing God's hand in everything and as providing all things allows us to believe He is working and that He will provide. We learn that those who spend time thanking Him are the ones who will see Him working, and so we will thank Him and praise Him all the more. Gratitude is powerful. Consider for just a moment what it's like to be on the receiving end of an unexpected expression of thanks. It surprises and delights us, and if I'm honest, I must admit that experience makes me eager to turn around and give again.

Our kids need gratitude. They need to see that God is working and moving in the world around them. While the news shouts loud about tribulation and destruction and hardship, we can marvel at how God is still faithful to us—always keeping His promises, always providing a way through, and always, always close. Our kids need to be taught that to praise and give thanks are prayers that can be offered anywhere. God can be seen and felt everywhere, from the colors of the changing leaves to the way the sun kisses their cheeks. They can be taught to find gratitude in soft exclamations of delight and even in what is hard. No detail is too small. James 1:17 tells us every good gift comes from the Father.

Again, those who watch for God's hand are the ones who see Him working. And when we see Him working we thank Him and praise Him all the more.

"Enter his gates with thanksgiving and his courts with praise; give thanks to him and praise his name. For the LORD is good and his love endures forever; his faithfulness continues through all generations" (Psalm 100:4-5 NIV).

Step Four: Intercession

I often rush to the *asking for what we need* part of prayer. Certainly we have times for that, but deliberately walking through praise, confession, and thanksgiving before intercession means we will likely have hearts filled with faith—faith being a key ingredient to answered prayer. Hebrews 11:6 tells us, "Without faith it is impossible to please God, because anyone who comes to him must believe that he exists and that he rewards those who earnestly seek him" (NIV). Faith is generated in us by considering the faithfulness of God, and because we see His faithfulness we ask convinced that He lovingly and willingly acts on our behalf. What a gift!

My friend Fern says, "An intercessor is simply someone who prays for another, one who pleads before God's throne on behalf of another." As the founder of Moms in Prayer International, she has a lot of experiential wisdom in this area. "An intercessor is not only one who stands in the gap but is also one who takes seriously her authority (her position) in Christ. She prays with confidence because she knows she has been made worthy by Jesus' blood, and she knows that praying in His name will pierce the darkness and cause the stronghold to tumble down. She remembers who she is and is secure in her identity—redeemed, saved by grace and dutifully standing between the need and her almighty God."[3] It's important that we remind our kids that because we are His children, the Lord has given us unlimited access to Him and no request is too big or too small.

While intercession is a term reserved for praying for others, this is a great time to teach your children to pray strategically for themselves. The method I have found most successful is to pray in ripples. My prayers begin with me, and then spread to those in my home, and then to those in my extended family and friends, then to our church and schools, then to our neighborhood, and then further outside our sphere. Some other areas to focus on both as a family and to cultivate in their individual prayer times might be

Teachers → *Principals* → *Friends* → *People who don't know the Lord*

Pastors → *Missionaries* → *Governors* → *Presidents*

Disaster → *Relief Teams* → *Refugees* → *Persecuted believers*

Obviously the possibilities are endless.

I've noticed that the words I pray often become the script that plays in the minds of my children and forms the mold of their prayers. One of my daughters prays first, second, and last for the safety of everyone and everything. I see and sense in my heart that my bent toward fear has become hers. While the world gives us plenty of reasons and opportunities to pray for safety, let's pay close attention to what we are modeling in prayer. When we are tempted to pray for safety and protection, let's also pray for the kingdom of light to advance. When our children's hearts quiver, let's pray for boldness, courage, and a steadfast reliance on the God who promises to tuck them under the refuge of His wings.

This year I had the opportunity to interview Stephen Kendrick, the cowriter and producer of the popular Christian movies *Courageous*, *Facing the Giants*, and *War Room*. Stephen told me as a child he would sometimes wake with a nightmare and feel afraid. His mom would come into the room, sit next to him, and pray Psalm 91 over him. She would boldly pray protection for her boy and fill his mind with truth. Then she would tell him to pray Scripture with her, out loud, on purpose.[4] The pattern she was developing in him was to fight fear with the offensive weapon of prayer, using God's Word.

Yes, we can and should pray for rest and protection, but these tender moments are opportunities to teach our children to run to the tower of the Lord and find refuge in Him through prayer. Our children's fear, and indeed our own, can and will be driven out as we learn to meditate on the character of God. Let's teach our kids to use the Word as the weapon it is meant to be.

Perseverance and Unanswered Prayers

If we pray, then we have no doubt experienced a time or many times when our prayers were either not answered immediately or not at all. Surprisingly, Jesus told His followers this would happen (Luke 18:1). In His sovereignty, God intends for us to pray about certain concerns for a long time. Perhaps that is for character shaping as we wrestle, or perhaps it's to clarify our motives. Whatever the case, sometimes we must persevere in prayer.

One tender example in our lives has been for the salvation of one of my closest family members. I remember the first night tears ran down my cheeks as I pled for the Lord to open his heart and allow him to turn to Christ. I was 20 years old the first time the desperation of the salvation of another wrecked me. It took 15 years to see that prayer answered, and I confess I sometimes believed it would never happen.

I have already seen tears down the cheeks of my children and heard their fervent prayers for someone's salvation. I am awed by the tenderness and depth of insight He has developed in them. They are capable of understanding so much more than we give them credit for, including times when the Lord says no.

We lost our friend Ryan to cancer despite the fervent, desperate prayers for healing from our family. My son, Brendan, lost his personal hero when we lost Ryan. The two were deeply invested in one another. In his final days, Ryan gave Brendan one of his signature cowboy hats, and tonight, four years after his death, my son left the house wearing it. I was afraid of what God's no might do to Brendan's faith—the faith of all of us, really. But we were given a grace for this "no" that I never saw coming. We experienced a deep understanding of God's goodness despite the loss that grew inside all of us. We knew pools of grief, but grace to carry us through. We can trust Him.

Our God listens and leans in when we pray, and we can know that teaching our kids to pray about everything will benefit them for a lifetime. Let's build patterns of prayer in their lives that give them the benefit of second-nature prayers. As Fern once told me, "Intercessors change history." Let's release thousands of world changers into the next generation.

> *Precious Lord,*
> *I desperately want my kids to become children who love prayer. Teach them through my example to "pray without ceasing," as we are told to do in 1 Thessalonians 5:17. And to approach Your throne of grace with confidence so they may receive mercy and find grace to help them in their time of need, as we are told will happen in Hebrews 4:16. Show me opportunities to weave prayer throughout our lives, and how to cultivate in my children a desire for communication with You. In Jesus's name, amen.*

Teach Them About Self-Control

Most powerful is he who has himself in his own power.
—SENECA

Saturdays at home are a rare treasure for our family. Normally, we have to rush out in the morning for basketball practice, a church gathering, chores on the farm, speaking events—you name it, we usually have something going on. I'd guess that for only two days a month, Mike and I wake up together, kiss good morning, and head downstairs for a leisurely time of coffee and catching up. I'm not complaining—I love the life God has built for us. I just want you to understand that this time is nearly sacred in my mind. Generally, we snuggle the kids one by one as they arrive bleary-eyed and disheveled from a good night's sleep.

Recently, however, Ryan, my six-year-old, arrived with energy bubbling over. It was entertaining for a few minutes to watch him wrestle his brother and pester his sister, but quickly it became more than I could bear on half a cup of coffee. Mike and I needed this time as a couple to reconnect and plan the weekend, so I turned to Ryan and said, "Ry, do you see that doorway? I need you to pretend there's an invisible wall right there and stay on the other side of it for a while."

Ryan looked at me, puzzled, apparently deeply pondering the ramifications of the boundary he had just been given. He left, but then a few minutes later he reappeared and interrupted us again. I quickly and sternly asked him where he was supposed to be, and he cocked his head to the side and looked at me as seriously as he could. "I'm sorry, Mom. I'm just not very good at invisible walls."

That'll preach.

Reckless Warriors

The idea that we would produce warriors ready for battle who don't practice self-control should be terrifying to us. There will be no righteous battle if our children don't learn to harness their minds, bodies, and emotions. Scripture is filled with people who lacked discretion and whose potential for godliness, leadership, and usefulness were cut short because of moral failure. Charles Spurgeon said, "Tiny foxes spoil the vineyards; and little sins do mischief to the tender heart."[1]

Consider for a moment that Esau forfeited his inheritance to his brother Jacob for a bowl of stew. Rather than wait an hour for servants to prepare dinner, he failed to practice self-regulation and gave away his precious right to the blessing of his father. Remember Samson, whose love for beautiful and ungodly women took a man God had set in leadership and destroyed him. No amount of strength in his body or gorgeous flowing hair could withstand the test of his self-control. Moses's anger problem, no matter how justifiable, kept him out of the promised land. King Saul, King David, and King Solomon faced devastating consequences during their reigns because they failed to tell themselves no. The list goes on and on.

Saying No to Ourselves

A few years ago, I spotted a *Christianity Today* magazine in a doctor's office. A popular musician was on its cover, and I grabbed it up and began skimming. I had made it to page 11 when I was stopped cold by an article title: "Spotlight: The Sex Lives of Unmarried Evangelicals." My first thought was *unmarried* evangelicals shouldn't be having sex, and my second thought was *I wonder how they define "evangelical."*

The article brought to light the devastating reality facing the church. These statistics say, "Christians are having premarital sex and abortions as much (or more) than non-Christians," while pointing out, as I suspected, that we had better get our hands around what evangelical really means.[2] One survey conducted by the National Campaign to Prevent Teen and Unplanned Pregnancy/Guttmacher Institute reported that 45 percent of those surveyed (ages 18–29) were currently in a sexual relationship, while another 34 percent had previously been in one. That left only 21 percent of those "unmarried evangelicals"—a staggering number—as celibate. The organization Gray Matter Research tightened the definition of an evangelical as one who attended church at least monthly and held to traditional evangelical beliefs on salvation, the Bible, evangelism, and active faith. It reported that only 10 percent of those surveyed even fit that criteria. Of that 10 percent, though, 56 percent of respondents reported they were celibate.[3]

Some of your eyes just glossed over. I get it. Numbers do that to me too. But here's what wouldn't let go of me that day. Using the most conservative numbers with the tightest definition of the word *evangelical*, almost half of our kids are caving to sexual temptation. Half of the good church kids. Go ahead and let that blow your mind too.

I started wondering if we simply do not know how to say no to ourselves. I'm not throwing stones here; I fell into this particular pit, and my guess is about half of you reading these words did too. But I wonder if we have brought this generation to a place where they haven't learned to deny themselves anything at all.

The "Y" in the Road

To develop self-control, our children need to learn to identify temptation. The picture of temptation I've begun to paint for my children and our youth group kids is the idea—or feeling—that we have a "Y" inside. Temptation is a moment when two choices lie in front of us. One decision or way is the path our "self" wants to go on. It looks appealing, it seems good, it may even be easier. The other way is the path we know would be better for us. I'm telling my kids temptation is the "Y" moment in the road with a pull to do something negative.

We all face temptation, and those temptations look different for each of us. Tonight my friend Cindy is taking an unofficial poll of her friends on Facebook for her upcoming book, asking them about the temptations they face and how they are overcoming them. (The timing is uncanny. I love when Jesus does things like this; He's such a kick.) As I read down the list of all the temptations these friends had already listed, I realized two things. One, the temptations always kicking me in the knees weren't listed! And two, a slew of temptations I don't struggle with were there—praise the Lord and hallelujah for it.

That's just it, though, isn't it? We can either try to develop a list of rules for our children to follow, or we can prepare them to listen to the prompting of the Holy Spirit because we don't know what temptations they might face. We need to tell them that when they feel that "Y" moment, they need to stop and listen.

The idea that there is a standard of right and wrong or even that one path is best is going to fly in the face of today's culture. Postmodernism says, "You get only one life. Do what makes you happy," "The only wrong choice you'll make is the one you let someone make for you," or even "You can make either decision. The only one who might be hurt is you." Parents definitely have an uphill battle if their kids are saturated in the culture we live in.

Scripture tells us in Romans that everyone is hardwired with a conscience. If we take God at His word, that means He has placed some kind of warning system in everyone that knows some things are definitely right and others are definitely wrong.

> Whether they recognize it or not, even those who have
> never been exposed to the revelation of God's Word are

instinctively aware of His existence and of His basic standards of righteousness. "They show that the work of the Law written in their hearts, their conscience bearing witness, and their thoughts alternately accusing or else defending them. In most societies of the world, even in those considered uncivilized...Men inherently know that such things as greed, envy, murder, deceit arrogance, disobedience and mercilessness are wrong."[4]

Part of the human condition is the reality of living in a sin-filled world, with cards stacked against holiness and with temptation to skirt the moral code written on our hearts. Conscience is the gift that points the way, but conscience alone is not enough to overcome temptation.

"No temptation has overtaken you except what is common to mankind" (1 Corinthians 10:13 NIV).

Temptation Unpacked

It's Normal

> Being tempted to act out in any of these ways and thousands of others is not sin. The decision that comes right after the temptation is the defining moment.

Unfortunately, teaching about temptations often fails to mention that being tempted isn't a sin, but a part of the human condition. It's helpful to remind our kids (and ourselves) that being tempted to swear, cheat, steal, and lie is not in itself sinful. Neither is having the desire for sexual fulfillment outside of marriage, being tempted to try drugs and alcohol, or even facing same-sex attraction. Being tempted to act out in any of these ways and thousands of others is not sin. The decision that comes right after the temptation is the defining moment.

It's Best Avoided

Although temptation is not sinful, willingly putting ourselves in an environment where we will face it over and over again shows a lack of wisdom. Parents should take notes through the first few chapters of Proverbs as King Solomon directs his son into wisdom and righteous living. As they considered the path of a wayward woman who is attractive and interested in seducing his son, Solomon reminded him, "Keep your way far from her, and do not go near the door of her house, lest you give your honor to others" (Proverbs 5:8-9).

The realities about premarital sex within young Christendom is proof that our kids are radically failing when they arrive at that spot in the road. In short, they should never have even been on that street. We must help them see that the destination would have changed completely if a thousand little choices prior to it were made differently.

Avoiding temptation includes a deep knowing of ourselves and our weaknesses. Avoiding places where we will face temptation also includes trying to avoid times when we know our minds spiral downward and rework the path.

It Involves Suffering

It would be a complete fallacy to believe facing temptation is easy. We paint the wrong picture when we say, "Just say no" or that it is easy on the other side of the temptation. For some, saying no is never easy, and the struggle lasts a lifetime. Breaking habits and facing addictions is hard. I've watched someone I love fight with everything in him to break a drug addiction. At some point, it really is easier just to cave and do the wrong thing. The results are devastating, but the immediate sense of relief is there. Hebrews 2:18 assures us that Christ knows the pain of temptation, and that "because he himself has suffered when tempted, he is able to help those who are being tempted." I take great comfort in the fact that Christ can relate, because it *is* hard.

As mothers, we must acknowledge that disciplining our children involves suffering. We experience very little pleasure in redirecting behavior, assigning consequences, and trying to identify underlying issues. The truth is this work is trying and can be exhausting. The world is full of parents who have struggled with their children but tapped out along the way, too exhausted to fight another battle. They are too distracted and too frustrated, and they assume the kinks will work themselves out along the way. The problem is three-year-olds who throw temper tantrums become teenagers who rage, respond disrespectfully, and manipulate others.

The only way we will faithfully stay the course in this area when we are worn thin is to believe that "for the moment all discipline seems painful rather than pleasant, but later it yields the peaceful fruit of righteousness to those who have been trained by it" (Hebrews 12:11). Our discipline does not indicate less love for our children, but rather our steadfast commitment to them. While it may take it out of us now to fight the small battles, we need to have our eyes on the fact that God promises peace, godly success, and an abundant harvest in our children if we dig deep now.

It Can Overtake Them

"No temptation has overtaken you that is not common to man" (1 Corinthians 10:13). It's so important to remember our children will face temptations they don't have the power to fight themselves. The word *overtake* means my children may face sins that could capture them and overpower them. I have seen godly people destroyed by addictions and ungodly relationships they believed they could control. However, some sins grab hold of us and are impossible to face in our own strength. In our humanity, we cannot fight or withstand all situations. That is why we have been given the Holy Spirit. The power of God in us is what gives us the ability to face temptation and respond with self-control. While the conscience may give us direction, the Holy Spirit gives us the power to act in godliness. Praise Him for the gift of the Spirit.

The Role of the Spirit

When the Spirit comes into our lives at the time of belief, He brings with Him fruit He will develop in believers who yield to Him. This promise is not age dependent and it has no physical limitations.

"The fruit of the Spirit is love, joy, peace, patience, kindness, goodness, faithfulness, gentleness, self-control; against such things there is no law" (Galatians 5:22-23).

Self-control is often used as a synonym for moderation, sensibility, reasonableness, self-discipline, soberness, and prudence. In the life of a believer, the Holy Spirit provides the iron in our souls necessary to stand when temptation storms the castle and threatens to undo us. He quickens our hearts when small decisions lead to great decisions. It is such a relief to know the battle inside us will not be won by our might or our power, but by the Holy Spirit (Zechariah 4:6). He is the one who produces self-control in us that leads to steadfastness (2 Peter 1:6).

Positively, self-control isn't just what we avoid, but what we do over and over again. Not all the self-control exerted in our lives will be avoiding, but rather setting up healthy patterns that lead to rewards. One positive act is building wisdom and discernment through regular consumption of the Word. Another is the determination to keep our bodies healthy and in shape so they may be used by God.

"If we live by the Spirit, let us also keep in step with the Spirit" (Galatians 5:25).

How Do We Teach Them?

Catch Them Doing It Right

Parents must applaud when children yield to their consciences, and they need to actively help them learn to identify moments when the Holy Spirit prompts them. For example, sometimes one of our children decides not to retaliate for an injustice. Big brother snags the iPad out of little sister's hands, and instead of yelling she lets it happen this time, extending unsolicited forgiveness and grace.

We can lean over and whisper, "You had a choice right then for how you would respond. You chose to be kind. I'm proud of you. That honored the Lord." Or perhaps your teenager tells you he's lost friends over his decision to avoid partying and locker-room talk. Recently, I've had the opportunity to discuss making countercultural decisions with my kids, and I've been reminded how much they need to hear us cheer when they make good decisions.

All our kids are voracious readers. When they were younger, it was easy to make sure I screened the books they were reading and addressed attitudes in the characters or plot developments that didn't line up with a Christian worldview. As they've grown, however, it has become impossible to pre-read all their books, and instead I've been forced to rely on the recommendation of other godly friends and the filter we've developed over the years.

Recently, two of my kids have brought books to me, concerned about the content. The first was my 11-year-old, who was reading a novel for preteens that talked about a boy falling in love with another boy. We'd pulled this one off the library's recommended reading shelves. It wasn't the way I would have chosen to start having conversations about homosexuality with my daughter, but I praised God and her that she had been thinking through what she was reading and wanted to talk with me about it. Further, recently an adult gave me a recommendation for our teenager, and after a light scanning of the book, Brendan handed it back and said, "I don't think it's a good idea for me to be reading this one." Upon further review, although it was in his favorite genre, the book contained several sex scenes. I thanked the Lord for guarding my 13-year-old's heart and for the early wisdom inside him that knew it was unwise to spend time reading about sexual encounters when he's trying to live a life of purity before the Lord.

Discipline Consistently

Inconsistency in discipline and response to sin is hugely confusing to our kids, and it doesn't reflect the love and discipline of our Father. When we respond with disproportionate anger over small things, we aren't modeling self-control; we are instead modeling erratic discipline. And when we fail to follow through on discipline and allow misbehavior to go unaddressed for stretches of time until we snap, we aren't modeling love either. There's another option as well, which is to turn a blind eye, perhaps most destructive of all. We need to lean into the Holy Spirit and walk in step with Him, consistently modeling the message of the gospel and the power of repentance, forgiveness, and grace.

Model Faithfully

Some things are learned best by watching others, and self-control is no exception. What is God calling you to say no to? Over the years, my children have watched me tackle small sessions of prayer and fasting. Fasting is a valuable tool for learning to say no to myself. While my fasts from food end within days, they have provided great opportunities to teach my children that we hunger for something greater than food.

I've already told you we eliminated television from our lives for several years. It was a decision to say no to something that would have entertained us, but TV was a distraction from spending that time playing and reading with our kids. Television allowed us to veg out instead of investing in each other. We have the fantastic opportunity of allowing them to see the struggle and reward of self-control up close if we're willing to allow our kids into that intimate space of our hearts.

Broken-Down Walls

"Like a city whose walls are broken through is a man who lacks self-control" (Proverbs 25:28 NIV).

Walls are built for protection. Just like Jerusalem was defenseless to her enemies before Nehemiah rebuilt the walls, so are we defenseless without self-control. The Enemy can sneak in and set up shop before we know it, threatening our lives, ruining our witness, and laying waste to our character, marriages, and families.

Even godly kids have weak moments. Recently, my kind, tenderhearted son was struggling with something unspoken. For the life of us, Mike and I could not figure out what was going on. At the beginning of the day we could tell something was eating at him, but by evening his emotions were bubbling over. He's usually joyful and filled with peace, but in an instant he snapped. His emotions raged hot, his tone grew sharp, and once he got going the volume level increased.

We were in the middle of a campground where everyone knows everyone's business, if you know what I mean. There we stood, completely baffled, as he wound tighter and tighter until he was shouting at his dad. It was clear that a dam had broken inside him, and soon the anger turned to deep, heavy sobs.

I pulled my big ole boy into my lap and let him cry. Mike walked over and put his arms around him too. Usually we're quick to respond to talking back and disrespect, but in this moment we knew our young hero was being dealt with by the Holy Spirit. He apologized and asked for our forgiveness, and soon fell asleep, exhausted from the emotion expended. The next morning we had one of the most weighty conversations of my mothering career, and it all revolved around Proverbs 25:28.

When we fail to exercise self-control and allow anger and emotions to run out of control, we experience devastating consequences. Chief among them are shame and guilt. My son could relate in that moment to the devastation of not addressing the small irritations correctly and instead allowing his emotions to run away with him. It was a precious time of reconciliation and a powerful lesson to me about the protection of the walls of self-control.

Mamas, we have the great responsibility of teaching our kids to respect the walls God has put into place in our lives. No one is born "good at invisible walls," as my son Ryan pointed out. The bending of our wills to the Lord is part of the process of making us look like Him. And we can be so thankful that He doesn't leave us alone to do the heavy lifting. The Spirit inside us will protect us and allow us to stand as a city on a hill, foundation intact.

Lord,

I believe Your Word and Your ways will protect my family. Help me to be faithful to train my children in the small moments so they will be ready to face temptations and trials in the future. Create in them a longing for wisdom and discernment so they can recognize traps from the Enemy. I'm grateful that You walk alongside them and will guide them in paths of righteousness, protecting their minds and hearts as they submit to You. Help me to teach them to use self-control. In Jesus's powerful name, amen.

15

Teach Them About Relationships

*God is more interested in your future and
your relationships than you are.*
—Billy Graham

I run in a social circle where we discuss behavior styles, personality types, and Myers-Briggs assessments in casual conversation. It's not unusual to see a quick roll of the eyes or a playful shove, along with a muttered, "Humph, introverts" or "You're such an *I*."

It delights me to no end that we were created for relationships, but I realize not everybody leaps at the chance to make new friends and deepen relationships. Rest assured that if you would rather be poked in the eye than have a touchy-feely conversation, you will be just fine in this chapter.

When we teach behavioral styles, we talk about the art of flexing. Flexing is allowing yourself to be stretched in an area you would typically avoid or that you believe is a weakness. As we discuss equipping our kids to be successful in relationships, we will have to take into account the idiosyncrasies and nuances of their personalities and encourage a healthy stretch to meet others where they are. From the very beginning it wasn't good for man to be alone, and so God gave Adam a wife, yes. But in that moment what He truly gave him was a companion and friend. When we're living life beside others we look like the Father.

Our kids are going to engage in so many types of relationships. They will be family members, friends, students, and members of the body of Christ. A word of caution as we begin? Relationships will look different for the next generation. When I was school age, I would take the cordless phone into my bedroom and talk to my friends for hours. Today I rarely talk on the phone, and even then I do it with a specific handful of people. My friends and I text constantly, something I despised even a few years ago but has now become a typical part of my day. This new development of adding screens to relationships will offer our children new opportunities to engage others, and as we well know, it will present an entire range of complications. Equipping them to navigate relationships in this next generation will require prayer and wisdom. May God give us both.

Real Friends

I was an ill-prepared mother. I don't know if I had ever held a newborn when my first child was born. I probably hadn't changed more than ten diapers in my life. Trying to conceive for two years had been my focus, but when I learned I was pregnant, reality hit. I was not one bit educated about what was going to happen to my body and my life, and I knew very little about how to care for a baby.

My first stop after learning of my pregnancy was my local Barnes & Noble, where I bought several books about pregnancy. A few days later I headed to a maternity shop in the mall just because I had earned the right to be in that store. I nearly hid when a saleswoman asked me when I was due. I mean, I was after all about 20 days post conception, but who's counting, anyway? I spent a fortune on cream to prevent stretch marks and lollipops that are supposed to stop nausea. Both were pie in the sky ideas.

What I didn't realize was that every twinge in my middle would leave me wondering if everything was okay inside me. I headed to a site that connected me to an online pregnancy board with hundreds of other mothers who were also due in July 2003. At first I just scoured the boards to learn if what I was experiencing was "normal," and I scoped out what would be happening in two or three weeks, because my due date was at the end of the month. Oh, the wisdom of those two weeks ahead of me. I so treasured that place of learning that I checked in every day.

Soon I was discussing my "friends'" pregnancies with Mike, deeply caring about their babies' well-being and reading their birth stories while crying my eyes out. As time passed, that group of hundreds of mothers shrank to a core group of about 30 women, and we decided to form our own little place out of the public's eye. The interesting part was that I felt ashamed to admit to my "real life" friends that I had "online" friends, but I knew some of the friendships I was forming were the real deal too.

The day came when one of my "board" friends wanted to meet up when she brought her family to our area. Of course, I'd never have met her alone, but Mike came with me and we had a fantastic time together as little families. We would eventually add friends and lose friends just like real life and schedule big gatherings and little gatherings. Four days before Mike and I went to meet Gabriella in Guatemala, my online friends pulled off a surprise party in Chicago. I felt so loved and valued. At that point these relationships were as real as real could be and very important to me. Today, four of the women on my regular prayer team are from that group, nearly 15 years later.

This is the problem with discrediting all online relationships or minimizing their worth in the lives of our young people. Real friendships can be created. Because of technology, our world has widened to people we would never have met or been able to connect with. I sit on my couch and communicate with friends in China, England, and a village in Indonesia where conditions are primitive. Gone are the days of camp pen pals who saw each other for only one week during the summer. My niece just told me her camp cabin communicates all the time now via group text. That thrills me to no end since they met at a Christian camp and made decisions to walk with the Lord and hold each other accountable. It's a gift.

But we all know this coin has a flip side. We've seen marriages wrecked as Facebook has opened the door to relationships with past flames. I know I spend time sucked into an online world that leaves me neglecting the one right in front of me, the people right next to me. We may complain about our kids and their hundreds of text messages, but the reality is I rarely have a conversation with my own friends when we don't answer texts or fiddle with our phones. We are in the middle of raising children in the digital age, and if most of us were honest, we'd have to admit we haven't developed a game plan or a philosophy for how our families are going to form relationships in this generation.

Instead of throwing up our hands in this area, let's recognize that digital relationships are just another type of relationship we all must steward. It's a complex and dynamic area because social media and technology are ever changing, but we can identify dangers right now and make our children aware of them.

Three Warnings About Digital Relationships and What to Teach Our Kids

The Screen Allows a Disconnect Between Action and Reaction

I've noticed that people are a little bolder when they respond on social media. Haven't you? Things I could never imagine coming out of someone's mouth seem to spill off their fingers as if without thought or being aware of the potential consequences. We've all seen this play out when someone types something and we think, *You would never have said that in person.* We have even developed a word for people who snark online anonymously: trolls. They're the ones who hide out of sight and take potshots at people from a distance.

Something about a screen seems to block us from recognizing a person is attached to the email address and a living, breathing human is behind the Twitter handle or avatar image. People. Real people who would give verbal and nonverbal feedback that would help hold our emotions in check during an encounter. We must teach our kids that this screen in front of them is not a shield but a magnifying glass. It doesn't protect anyone. Sharp words thrown across the internet or typed on their phones hurt real people. In a face-to-face encounter, we can hear tone, inflection, and emotion in a voice, and we watch the physical reaction of our words upon the person. That's missing behind the screen. Where school-place bullying once happened in a stagnate place like a locker room or hallway, now it can occur on a real-time, real-world stage. To that end, acting as the magnifier it is, bullying can make evil and wickedness appear even more common than it is.

It's easy to fill a newsfeed with anything these days. It takes courage to look up and take real stock of the world around us through experience and at people rather than what people want us to see.

Let's Teach Our Kids Instead: All People Are Valuable

Imagine with me what would happen if our kids understood that all lives have worth simply because God made them.

> God created man in his own image, in the image of God he created him; male and female he created them (Genesis 1:27).

> This is what the LORD says—your Reedemer, who formed you in the womb (Isaiah 44:24 NIV).

Do you believe that, brave mama? Do you believe that inside every human being is the image of God that marks his or her worth? Do you believe that, as Isaiah says, God formed us in our mothers' wombs and that anything formed by God's hand has infinite worth? It's important that we believe this truth to our core and teach it to our children. We all have worth because we were created by our Creator. That means short people have worth and tall people have worth.

Red, yellow, black, white, brown, and freckled. Americans and Algerians. Communists and those under democracy. Certainly male and female. Undoubtedly the poor and the rich. Muslims, Hindus, Buddhists, atheists, and witch doctors. Don't flinch, now, because it's all true and we must stare this concept of worth unflinchingly in the eye. All people have value, and that includes those who love us and those who persecute us—or simply drive us crazy. That means we need to constantly reorient our feelings back to the truth, that God values people and we need to value them, too, even if all we can find in common is the image of God marked on us.

Throwaway words don't exist. That's a myth. James 3:6 says the tongue is a fire and with it we can set the whole course of our lives aflame. What a disservice we do for our children if we don't address the root of an issue that can burn their lives right down. That wild and reckless little tongue holds in it the power of life and death (Proverbs 18:21), and learning to restrain it is the proof of wisdom.

Where in the world do we start as parents? First, we watch the words coming out of our own mouths and typed by our own fingers. Remember, our example speaks louder than our words ever will. If my words slander or tear down others, which includes tongue-lashing our children, our kids will follow suit.

Second, call out our children on reckless, destructive words. They have no place in the life of a child of God. "With the tongue we praise our Lord and Father, and with it we curse human beings, who have been made in God's likeness. Out of the same mouth come praise and cursing. My brothers and sisters, this should not be" (James 3:9-10 NIV). Every word brings a reaction. They will either build up or tear down, and sometimes we need to let our children see us slack-jawed by the unkind words they say or write. I don't want my kids to be silent when they see others ganging up; I want them to be the ones who have the courage and pluck to say, "That's wrong. Knock it off!"

Last, we must help them look for ways to build up others. This kind of thing is countercultural and unnatural. A well-placed "thank you" or encouraging word is worth its weight in gold.

Screens Have a Remarkable Way of Revealing Self-Absorption

Full disclosure: I took selfies before selfies were a thing. This pre-dated selfie sticks, which by the way, I saw in a church in Haiti, proving Americans have infected the entire world. Anyway, this was back in the days of rolls of film you left at the grocery store and got photos a week later. If I wanted a picture of myself in any setting I had to take it myself.

We want to make memories and keep them forever. I have a gillion scrapbooks to prove it. However, if a person handed me a stack of pictures they took of themselves every day, then their pride, self-centeredness, and self-fixation would be obvious. It never occurred to me that the world would want to see me standing in front of a mirror with my lips pursed. Now, however, we're all able to star in our own little reality show, and, well, the results are noxious. There's a fine line here, and I'm not sure I know where it is, but I think it's safe to say our children can get caught in a social media trap that allows their egos to be stroked or shattered by the number of comments or likes on a page.

Let's Teach Our Kids Instead: Influence Must Be Stewarded Wisely

Social media has given us access to instant platforms. Our one fantastic life will point to something, but will it point to us or to Jesus? It's difficult to discern how much of our posting is acting like a scrapbook of our life and when it crosses the line into self-exultation. When it comes down to it, our motives will be weighed by the Lord (Proverbs 16:2), but while we have our children's ears, let's ask some good questions that might help reveal their heart condition.

Before letting them sign up for the next social media platform, ask them what their motivation is and set a standard of conduct. Address the temptation to push the envelope with words and pictures, and for heaven's sake remind them this stuff is permanent—as in they will likely revisit it at a job interview permanent. Remind them people will be watching and that they will have the opportunity to use their voices to encourage or to discourage, to talk about themselves, or to highlight others and Jesus. Some young people are doing a fantastic job at this.

One of my heroes is Katie Davis Majors. She was 18 years old when she first visited Uganda and fell in love with the children. Her heart broke with the wounds and needs she saw—children without families, children without the hope of an education, children without food. I imagine she, much to her parents' dismay, heard the voice of God calling her to not only stay in the African nation, but to make a move to foster and finally adopt 13 beautiful girls. Her obedience required heroism not only from Katie, who laid down her life, but heroism from her parents, who let her go.

Katie gained a platform she never expected as the world watched and wondered why a beautiful girl would give up the American dream and potentially the hope of marriage to live and serve the least of these. Katie began a blog called "Kisses from Katie" as a way of connecting with home, but it soon shared the needs of the people she was meeting. She began using the platform God gave her to point others toward Jesus and His heart, to follow Him and love like Him. This has led to the development of an incredible ministry that feeds and educates hundreds of students. Katie's powerful witness uses the voice she has been given, leading countless others to love like Jesus and serve the broken. That's the power of using your platform to point to Jesus, folks. And we should all take note.[1]

Screens Allow Us to Walk Away from Conflict in Relationships

Our social media world makes unfriending someone sterile. If we don't appreciate their perspective, attitude, or even their frequency in addressing us, we can click a button and mute them from our world. Disagreements fade into the background and conflict is avoided by ignoring another. I'm not suggesting everyone gets to be our children's friends or even that our children shouldn't have the option of walking away from destructive relationships. I'm concerned that our attitude toward others becomes calloused and indifferent rather than longsuffering and loving. Because here's the truth: real relationships require work.

Let's Teach Our Kids Instead: Horizontal Relationships Affect Our Vertical Relationship

The word *fellowship* sounds like a Baptist church potluck in my mind. But fellowship is not just fruit plates, layered salads, and homemade cakes. In Scripture, fellowship means depth of relationship, intimacy, and building up others. While our children and maybe us, too, are tempted to believe fellowship happens merely between people, or between ourselves and God, we would be wrong. In 1 John 1, verses 3 and 7 tell us our fellowship is with the Father and the Son and with others. Imagine with me a triangular relationship where God is the point of the triangle at the top. His relationship is unbroken with us on one side and with others on the other side. Sin creates static in the line between us and the Father, but because of Christ's sacrifice, the line is never severed. Yet the fellowship, depth of relationship, and intimacy are certainly affected.

On the other side of the base of the triangle is our relationship with others. When we operate in the light, loving and serving others, forgiving each other, and building each other up, our triangle of fellowship with the Father flows unhindered. When we sin against one another, however, that adds static to the line between us *and* our relationship with the Father. "If we say we have fellowship with him while we walk in darkness, we lie and do not practice the truth. But if we walk in the light, as he is in the light, we have fellowship with one another, and the blood of Jesus his Son cleanses us from all sin" (1 John 1:6-7).

To believe our anger, resentment, and disharmony are kept just between us people is erroneous thinking. God takes that stuff personally. It really is all connected. Our kids must see that the way they treat others is a reflection of their hearts and that the Lord has an investment in our relationships with others. No sharp words to their siblings or parents or careless treatment of their neighbors occur without their fellowship with the Lord taking a hit. Fortunately, we can make that right time after time because of Christ.

Friendships

Where would superheroes be without their sidekicks? As we raise children to honor and seek the Lord, we must teach them about the power of friendships. I'm an extrovert married to an introvert, and we have two introverted children and two extroverted children. Some of my best friends are introverted and others are extroverted, but we all agree we need friendships.

We need the comfort that comes in sharing history and being known. We need people who will wade into the middle of our stuff with us and help us fight our way through. We need those who know our kryptonite, what would easily destroy us, and lead us in the opposite direction. We need loyalty, trust, mercy, forgiveness, and companionship in the journey. We need people who run beside us and tell us we can finish this race and help strengthen our wobbly knees. We need people who will drag us to Jesus when we lose our vision or our heart breaks. Introverts and extroverts alike, we need good friends, and our children do too.

The Enemy hates healthy friendships. It seems obvious to me that it's easier to target people who feel isolated and alone. Friends are the ones who detect that something suspect is going on when we begin struggling with doubt, fear, and shame. It seems only reasonable, then, that the Enemy would do anything to keep solid relationships from forming and even cast them in a suspect light. Our kids have a deep-seated need for same-sex friendships filled with love and richness. Recently, I took a picture of my daughter with her best friend. The two were walking down a path holding hands and smiling.

I remember those days from my childhood, and I remember times when I ached from the lack of a friend. Friendship is powerful, and without a doubt, friends can make or break a believer's faith walk.

When we consider what our kids need to know about healthy friendships, let's give them fantastic examples. Let's read them stories of powerful friendships like David and Jonathan's. We need to talk to them about Jonathan's choice to lay aside himself, his perceived rights to a throne, and love David, the Lord's anointed. They need to know being a good friend sometimes means giving encouragement when our friends are weak. Jonathan risked his own life to go see David at his very lowest and give him courage and strength. Tell them godly friendships call out the best in each other. Proverbs 27:17 says, "Iron sharpens iron, and one man sharpens another." Scripture tells us bravery is associated with true friendship. Friends must be willing to confront each other, give good advice, turn each other back from sin, encourage one another, and help carry each other's load. Those are huge responsibilities.

We must also prepare our children for the changing dynamics of friendship. If you're anything like me, you've experienced your fair share of temporary and seasonal relationships. It's important to remember, especially in middle school when our kids are at the height of the craziness, that friendships take time and good ones are a treasure. Explain the truth to them that sometimes we have to let people go, and that it's hard. To that end, we know poor choices in relationships can be the demise of our character. Choosing the right friends is crucial.

Remember Amnon and Tamar? Before Amnon's fatal choice to rape his sister, he was egged on by a friend name Jonadab. Second Samuel tells us Jonadab was a crafty man, and he helped Amnon devise a plan to lure Tamar. I can guarantee Jonadab's shady character had been revealed to Amnon before this shocker, but Amnon didn't flee.

Our children must learn to "not be deceived" because "'bad company ruins good morals'" (1 Corinthians 15:33). Our warnings will always be better received before our children are in the middle of a mess, but if we feel the catch of the Spirit over their friendships, it would be wise to make mention of that early.

Being BRAVE About Their Relationships

> Easy isn't BRAVE. It isn't going to train and equip my children to live courageously in a lost and hurting generation. Easy only prepares them for easy.

The plan for the advancement of the gospel today is the same as it was 2000 years ago. It involves relationships. While we want to teach our kids to choose their closest friendships wisely, we must remember that Christ's plan for salvation will require us not to be insular, but open-armed toward those who do not know Him. That means, as entire families, we need to be open to new relationships for the purpose of sharing the gospel, befriending people not as a means to an end, but engaging them out of love for them. If I view relationships this way, it transforms how I do everything. My conversations are intentional, where I sit at sporting events is intentional, and the love showered on other people's kids is intentional.

In the past we've hosted barbecues for our kids' elementary school classes complete with families. Before you imagine that we squeezed more than 60 people into our modest home, you need to know we set up tables outside to pull the whole thing off. Intentional friendship building has meant coaching soccer teams and loving kids who are real stinkers. We've hosted Christmas parties complete with cookie decorating and telling the real Christmas story. When we did this, I invited the moms to come with their daughters and enjoy the fun. That time was precious. The girls frosted and sprinkled cookies, and their moms and I enjoyed coffee together. When I read the Christmas story, there were no pulled punches, the moms heard the story of the Savior's birth right alongside their daughters. It was the perfect opportunity to let the girls ask good questions and learn more. My favorite one, "Well, if Jesus came on Christmas, why do we do Easter?" We couldn't have planned that moment better if we tried. At the end of the night the girls and I thanked the Lord for the way He orchestrated the whole afternoon. The connections we made during those times gave us common ground and built relationships I'm still drawing on years later.

This sounds like really big stuff, but if you could see my heart you'd know I would always prefer easy and less fuss. Easy would be having only my family in my home. Easy would be allowing my kids to have over only kids whose families love Jesus and who seem safe. But easy isn't BRAVE. It isn't going to train and equip my children to live courageously in a lost and hurting generation. Easy only prepares them for easy. Lost people aren't easy, but they are worth it.

Father,
Relationships are hard and sometimes painful. Please teach my children to love, accept, and encourage those around them. Develop in them a heart that treats others the way they would like to be treated. Allow Christ Jesus to be our example. I pray for my children's friends, that our family will be a beacon of light for them, pointing them to Jesus. Help my kids to love difficult people and rely on Your strength to do it. In Jesus's name, amen.

16

Teach Them to Serve

*I have learned that I will not change the world. Jesus
will do that. I can, however, change the world for one
person. So I keep stopping and loving one person
at a time. Because this is my call as a Christian.*
—KATIE DAVIS

It had been a hot five days in Haiti, and we were all resting when I heard the little bell jingling on the street below. We'd heard it a couple of times a day all week, and I knew who was walking by below our balcony—the shoe shiner.

I had seen shoe shiner stations in American airports, where businessmen stopped and read papers while someone buffed up their shoes. Kind of like a pedicure for men, only they forfeit the foot rub. Their loss. Cephas had told me at breakfast that the shoe shiners in Haiti are one step from the bottom rung of the social ladder. They travel the streets with their little wooden boxes, hoping to earn the equivalent of a quarter for a shoe shine. Who needs a shoe shine in a neighborhood where people have only one meal a day? I ran to the window, and then to Cephas.

"Brother, come on! He's here now. I want to meet a shoe shiner!" I said. Cephas smiled at me. "Yes, sister. Let's meet a shoe shiner." We walked down the cement stairs and the guard opened the gate. My brother leaned out of the gate and waved the bell-jingling man over to us. As he stepped through the gate and into the courtyard of the mission house, he looked surprised to see me and more than a little sheepish. Cephas handed him his black, American dress shoes, that were indeed in need of a good shine, and told the tall, bony man I wanted to meet a shoe shiner. The man nodded at me and smiled, set down his crate, and sat on it. He took out his tools and began to polish. The whole process took longer than I anticipated—it really does take a lot of elbow grease to make a pair of shoes shine.

While the shiner worked on one shoe, Cephas picked up the other. "I want you to teach me how to shine my shoes," Cephas explained. Cephas knelt beside him and watched the shiner brush, apply cream, and buff with expert hands. In the meantime, I noticed our new friend had on a faded black T-shirt with an American Christian cliché written on it. I wondered if he even knew what his shirt said, and so I asked him. "You are wearing a shirt that talks about Jesus. Are you a Christian? Do you walk with Jesus?" He looked up at me from the crate and stopped the buffing. "Yes, I am a Christian. I have been for many years now. I was baptized and I attend the church up the road."

I smiled, delighted and full. "Cephas, tell him that we are family, all three of us. We are brothers and sisters in Christ." Cephas smiled at us from the dirt where he knelt beside our shoe-shining brother. Our new friend talked to us about learning to shine shoes and finished with a sparkle in his eye. Cephas continued scrubbing from his knees and engaging the man in precious dialogue about life and faith. Each one leaned over to admire the other's work. It was a holy moment.

As the shoe shiner rose to leave, he thanked us for the opportunity to work, and as Cephas gave him the equivalent of two and a half days' wages for the job, he departed with a gleam in his eye. We agreed later that we had all needed that moment, kneeling together with the shoe shiner. I had seen Jesus in both men—the shoe shiner as he treasured

Jesus in a job that requires great humility, and in Cephas as he knelt and polished beside the shiner, giving him dignity and respect.

The memory reminds me so much of that moment at the Last Supper when Jesus knelt with the towel and basin and washed His disciples' feet.

> When he had washed their feet and put on his outer garments and resumed his place, he said to them, "Do you understand what I have done to you? You call me Teacher and Lord, and you are right, for so I am. If I then, your Lord and Teacher, have washed your feet, you also ought to wash one another's feet. For I have given you an example, that you also should do just as I have done to you" (John 13:12-15).

The thing about Jesus was that He seemed to have no respect for human hierarchy. While He could have sat with kings or wealthy men, He chose to work among common, broken, suffering, messy people. He had nothing to gain in reputation, esteem, finances, or platform from those around Him. Indeed, their attention or gifts could add nothing to the One who helped create the world, who owns the heavens and all that moves on the earth. Jesus knelt with nothing to gain and washed the feet of the riffraff band gathered around him.

Then He rose, sat back down, and told them, "A new commandment I give to you, that you love one another: just as I have loved you, you also are to love one another. By this all people will know that you are my disciples, if you have love for one another" (verses 34-35).

This is how the world will know we follow Christ: when we supernaturally and sacrificially love one another. Training and proving ground for a hero is sacrificial, selfless love. Our kids will never look or sound more like Jesus than when they're valuing people with the same value system the Lord used, and sacrificially serving them out of love for the Father. Service, then, is built as we consider the needs of others and reckon we can do something about them.

> Service assesses the needs of others, considers
> what they need, and meets that need to the best of
> the ability of the one who serves.

Just as with Jesus's service, some of people's most moving acts of
service come as love spills over into action. For example, when Brendan was only six years old, my husband had an extensive knee surgery.
Dozing after surgery on our couch, Mike woke up to find himself covered with a quilt and Brendan's two favorite teddy bears nestled in his
arms. Unbeknownst to either of us, our son sized up the situation and
decided that if he were in the same situation, he would need a blanket and the things that brought him the most comfort. That's what
service does. It assesses the needs of others, considers what they need,
and meets that need to the best of the ability of the one who serves.

I found myself on the receiving end of this kind of love one evening as I was settling my kids for bed. It had been a full day of camping, swimming, and bonfires, and I covered them up and sat down
between the two sets of bunkbeds in the camper to talk and pray.
As I looked up at my oldest two sitting on the top bunks, my son's
folded pocket knife slipped off the end of his bed and crashed into
my mouth. The pain was fierce and blood spilled out of my split lip.
Before I could even get my wits about me, all four kids set into motion.
One went for a wet cloth and ice, two were sizing up my injury, and
one was rubbing my back tenderly. It was a humbling moment on
so many levels, and as I walked out to the campfire that night with a
fat lip and some ice, I considered what had just happened. Service is
born out of compassion, empathy, and love. The pain had been worth
being on the receiving end of such lavish love.

Motive and Modeling

We begin modeling the heart of a servant the moment someone
places our child in our arms. Motherhood itself requires sacrifice and
putting someone else's needs ahead of our own. Without realizing it
we put their schedules, desires, and comfort first. I vividly remember

patting my oldest on the bum as he fell asleep until my wrist was sore and my arm ached. When Gabi came home from Guatemala and we were in the initial stages of transitioning, everything made her anxious. We all but stapled her to our sides for six months, making sure she knew she was ours and dearly loved. I've warmed cocoa for 44 exact seconds because that is the magic number, eliminated green peppers from dishes, pulled almost-out teeth, and cleaned up vomit.

Motherhood has service built right into it. But that doesn't mean my motive for serving was for the glory of God or that my attitude about serving in any way resembled Christ's. It seems that when the apostle Paul calls us to "be imitators of God, as beloved children." And "walk in love, as Christ loved us and gave himself up for us, a fragrant offering and sacrifice to God" (Ephesians 5:1-2), that probably means my grumbling to my husband at the distribution of night wakings, trips to town, loads of laundry folded, or papers signed is not the imitation of Christ He desires.

Knowing we exert the first and arguably the most powerful impression on our children, how can we begin modeling wholehearted service to them and train them to do the same?

Study Jesus Together

The New Testament is filled with stories about Jesus serving. When I delve into the stories of His interaction with people, I begin to see patterns and trends.

Jesus Saw People's Needs

Time and again, Scripture tells us Jesus was moved with compassion. He saw the widow who lost her only son and went to her in compassion, saying, "Do not weep" (Luke 7:13). When Jesus teaches the parable of the good Samaritan, He says it was compassion that made him move and bind up the beaten man (Luke 10). He sees the hunger of the crowd and tells the disciples He doesn't want to send them away hungry (Matthew 15). Moved with compassion, He heals those with diseases and blind men, and sees their spiritually lost condition

(Matthew 14,20; Mark 6). In an age when we're tempted to become indifferent to suffering and calloused to other's pain, Jesus's heartache moves us and motivates us deeply. We have an opportunity to ask our children strategic questions to begin teaching them to *really see* the needs of those in front of them. For example, when we hear about a tragedy or a natural disaster, we can ask them, "What do you think those people need right now?" When we see people grieving or in pain, we can ask, "What do you think would bring those people comfort?" Even better is helping our children act on some of those ideas. Let's train them to truly observe the people around them.

Jesus Touched People

When it came to healing people, Jesus had the authority and power to simply speak the word, and He did on occasion. Most healings, though, involved Jesus touching the lepers, making mud for blind eyes, touching the feverish, laying hands on the paralyzed, and welcoming kids into His arms. I want to be like that and I want my kids to be like that.

When I was in my early twenties, I helped lead a youth mission team to an orphanage in Russia. When kids needed patching up after a soccer game or hopscotch fall, they would come to me for cleaning up. On one occasion a boy fell and skinned his knee. It was one of those falls accompanied by gravel and his wound needed a good cleaning. I was trying to put on a pair of latex gloves when my friend walked in. He leaned over, grabbed a gauze pad, knelt before the boy, and began doctoring. No significant words passed between the two of us about the incident, but it's still a vivid memory in my mind. Universal glove precautions aside, I had made the choice that I didn't want the blood of a child I didn't know on my hands. All I could think was that I didn't want something to happen to me. My thoughts weren't on the boy in front of me or the pain of his wound.

Jesus wasn't like that, my friends. He simply wasn't like that. The memory of my selfish thoughts remain fresh, and I'm grateful that since then the Lord has given me many more opportunities to love with open arms and get dirty. There really is something profound about being touched.

Jesus Saw the Marginalized

Jesus stopped to talk to people whom others overlooked. He saw Zacchaeus the crook in a tree, He met a Samaritan woman at a well in the heat of the day, and He turned to look a bleeding woman in the eye. It would be easy to imagine that Jesus would spend His time in the Special Ed room at a school, in a hospital waiting room, or among the cots in a homeless shelter. He would plan a visit to the shanty towns of Haiti, or India, or Brazil. Jesus would share dinner with migrant workers around campfires and offer blankets to refugees. That's just who He is.

Jesus Taught Others

Serving someone well can also mean teaching life skills, speaking truth, and sharing the gospel. Does your family or child have a special skill that would benefit others? Instructing someone else in that skill can be serving too.

Show Them Messy

Ministry is messy. When it comes to teaching our children how to serve others, we must not shy away from showing them the less glamorous parts of service. True story: One of my favorite things to do is to take my children to visit the local nursing home where their grandma works. One of the benefits is that they sometimes get to experience talking with people who have tubes poking out of their noses, drool on their chins, or urine bags attached to their wheelchairs. I always try to remind them in the car before we head in that the people inside love children and miss their families. We can be Jesus to them when we look them in the eye, smile, and say hello. Honestly, I'm not sure who feels better about those smiles and words of greeting, especially from my littlest. We are all tickled. Your visits could include caroling on holidays, playing those squeaky band instruments, or hosting unofficial piano recitals. Just seeing young people is a joy for the residents and an opportunity for our families to value others and serve in love.

Serving others for the glory of God is rarely comfortable for us. In our home, serving has meant loving people far beyond the end of our dinner. It means entering the dysfunction that happens in the lives of people who have not yet met the changing power of Christ. The time involved in their lives may be marked by days and even months rather than hours and minutes. For us, that has meant taking a meal to a young mom I thought was strung out on drugs and then following up with bags of groceries when I saw her fridge was empty. It has meant sitting at sports events with parents who swear like sailors. It has meant our kids giving up their room for a night to a girl who had run away from home (her parents knew where she was), and they have played and helped care for kids who have never, ever been disciplined.

It has meant loving people whose lifestyles flew in the face of what we see in God's Word and hugging an uncle fresh out of jail. You see, when we are loving, serving, and reaching others for Christ, it will inevitably be outside our comfort zones. We need to do this in ways that are responsible and consider our family's safety, but I'm finding that after years of framing for our children the situation we've found ourselves in, they are learning to love like Jesus.

Our children also need to see poverty up close. Mike and I met in college in Chicago and fell madly in love in the Windy City. Moody Bible Institute, the college we attended, is situated in the heart of downtown, interestingly placed on the edge of one of the wealthiest districts in America but also mere blocks away from what used to be one of the most dangerous housing projects. The contrast was enough to give you whiplash. As the kids have grown, we've made frequent trips to downtown Chicago to take in the museums and the city's charm.

On one of the first trips we made with them downtown, we

encountered a homeless man with a handwritten sign asking for money. We'd barely crossed the street when Brendan stopped cold right in front of the man. Our tiny six-year-old looked at him and then looked up at us. The whole time, the dirty, disheveled man never lifted his eyes off the ground. Knowing our Brendan was full of questions and that if we didn't move him on we'd be answering them in front of the man, we tugged his hand to follow us. Not half a block down the street our tenderhearted boy started in.

"Mom and Dad, we need to go back. We have to go back! That man is hungry and he doesn't have food. He was dirty and he doesn't have a home. Aren't we going to help him?" As we rounded a street and sat down at a bagel shop to eat, nothing tasted good. We began explaining the vastness of the homeless community in Chicago, and some of the tricky aspects of helping with cash, but in the end we returned to where the dirty, hungry man had been sitting and found no sign of him. We were all heartbroken.

The thing about poverty is that it exists nearby. You just have to look for it. And two of the interesting by-products of interacting with those in poverty are the gratitude and compassion that grow inside us as we see others with less. If my trips into poverty-laden countries have taught me anything at all it's that everyone has something to give. I desperately want my children to give and serve others lavishly for the glory of God and to see themselves as able to serve right now with the skills, abilities, and possessions they have. But the truth is our temptation is to see the messy of the broken and hurting and the vastness of problems around the world and feel hesitant to engage. In withholding our resources, we teach our kids, whether or not we mean to, that they are not responsible for meeting those needs. I don't ever mean that, and I suspect you don't either.

> By this we know love, that he laid down his life for us, and
> we ought to lay down our lives for the brothers. But if any-
> one has the world's goods and sees his brother in need, yet

closes his heart against him, how does God's love abide in
him? Little children, let us not love in word or talk but in
deed and truth (1 John 3:16-18).

The truth is we just need to start. I heard Lysa TerKeurst say, "Do
for one what you wish you could do for all."[1] That thought has permeated my thinking. Start with one act of service for one person and
God will show you what to do next.

Teach Them to Look for the Corners

In any room full of people, generally some are in the center chat-
ting, laughing, and engaging with others. In my experience, however,
someone is usually sitting in a corner, if not standing alone or leaning against a wall. This is true in our children's classrooms, at their
lunch tables, in school locker rooms, at school dances, and in college
lecture halls. It's even true in churches. While this is certainly easier
for some of us than for others, we can train our children to look for
people on the outskirts and encourage them to do their best to stand
alongside them. This is a little known, yet transformative ministry
our children can have.

Just last night at our dinner table, my daughters were discussing
a girl in their class whom people tease relentlessly. It broke my heart
to hear the words her peers were saying to her. They told me it made
them sad for that precious little girl. We had a great conversation
about being the one who smiles at this girl, sits next to her, and draws
her out. Honestly, these people in the corners of the rooms are often
the first to accept Christ as we serve them with our friendship, because
they already know loneliness and a need in their heart.

Consider Others

When Jesus told His followers to do to others as they would like
done to them (Luke 6:31), He gave us cause to add a delay to our
days. This means when I encounter another person, I need to mentally ask myself a few questions. First, how would Jesus respond to this

person? Inevitably the answer would be "lovingly." Then, how would I like to be treated if I were this person? The answer to this question should always be age-related, because although we can identify how we would like to be engaged, someone older or younger might want something different. Last, what is the other person feeling in this moment? This requires our children to put themselves in someone else's shoes and consider their inner needs. We can shepherd our children through this process when the pressure is off and build confidence in them to act even when it won't be simple.

My parents were terrific at teaching us to serve others, and they started in our home. When we were very young, we played a game leading up to Christmas called "Secret Elves." Go on, roll your eyes. But my parents would have us all draw a name out of a hat and do one secret thing to delight or please another member of our family that night. The genius part was that not only did it teach us to serve others, but we began to consider the perspective of another. For instance, Mom loved baths, and I remember drawing a hot bath and leaving a love note next to it. And I remember turning down Dad's side of the bed and laying out pajama pants for him.

Recently, my kids were on the receiving end of thoughtful service. A precious "secret friend" brought over jar after jar of canned soups and salsas. They simply appeared on the shelves in our basement. If asked why this happened, the children would give you two reasons. One, this friend loves us and loves to serve (because who in their right mind works that hard on preserving food for someone else unless they are a servant), and two, because Mama is busy writing and didn't have a garden this year. But the most important aspect of the gift is that those jars in our basement emulate the giver's lavish and thoughtful love of Christ and elicited a response in our hearts of gratitude to God for His provision.

We can raise heroes by pointing out real heroes to our children. Servants take all forms, have all kinds of different giftings, and come from all kinds of different backgrounds. That's fantastic, because no two of our family members are alike. They will each be drawn to serve differently, and when we teach them the motivation and key components of serving well, they will begin to serve in ways we would have never imagined.

The Moment in Front of Us

Serving like Christ and bringing God glory have everything to do with the moment in front of us, the right now. If we begin asking the Lord to bring about situations where we can teach our children how to serve like Jesus, our days will overflow with opportunity. And what a light that will be! Even the frantic, secular world occasionally notices someone serving in humility and marvels. That's because serving is otherworldly. It looks nothing like the culture racing around us, encouraging us to look out for ourselves, hoard, and protect what's ours. In Christ, God gave us an example that truly is innovative and refreshing.

Service rolls up its sleeves and gets busy sharing the burden of work. Let's not underestimate the witness of our children jumping in and helping adults around them. That can mean stacking chairs as a family after a school event, hanging around a few extra minutes to help a coach pick up equipment after practice, or even being at school a few minutes early so they can help a teacher pass out papers or sharpen pencils. Servers are the grease that make every event happen, so let's point them out while we go about our days, and applaud our kids when they serve with a helpful heart.

Recently, my son rounded up three empty carts at the grocery store and pushed them into the coral. It was thoughtful and unprompted. Another of my kids stood up to a bully on behalf of another child. And another wrote a letter to one of our Compassion International kids, who lives in Guatemala. If no one else saw them serving like Jesus, I did. If no one else on God's green earth praised Him for it, I did. And all that, my friend, keeps me humbly aware of my need to lead by example and keep my eyes peeled for ways to serve.

Father,

Thank You for the example of Jesus, who came not to be served but to serve. Will You grow in my family a heart for serving like You did, loving like You did, touching others like You did, and bring glory to Yourself through it? Create in my children eyes to see the needs around them and a willingness to respond promptly and thoughtfully. In Jesus's name and for His glory, amen.

17

Teach Them to Find Their Identity in Christ

*If you are not attaching your identity to the unshakable
love of your Savior, you will ask the things in your
life to be your Savior. And it will never happen.*
—PAUL DAVID TRIPP

"Mini me"—that's what they rightly call her. The fact that my youngest daughter is the spitting image of her mother brings me delight and terror in the same breath. I find myself marveling as I comb the tangles out of her stick-straight hair that feels just like mine. She loves to look through my clothes and would choose items even trendier if I'd let her. She devours books, loves her people hard, worships with her eyes closed, and is eager to please. All those things are terrific. However, run just a little faster than her, and her competitive nature comes out. And when I say competitive, I mean her theme song may be "Anything you can do I can do better." Most of the time I can laugh it off, but occasionally it scares me.

This last year has been a tough one for me. Health battles caused me to pick up an extra 15 pounds, and I began to see changes in my body shape. For the first time in my life, I became obsessed with how

I looked. The fat talk started, I began obsessing about getting in runs, and I was constantly seeking affirmation. I spent an obscene amount of money on a pair of blue jeans. I became so desperate to change something about myself that I got a haircut. Newsflash: only in the movies do haircuts fix insecurity issues.

Eventually I began to let my close friends in on the struggle in my mind, and the Lord began to heal my heart. If I learned anything in that period of time, though, it was that insecurity can make us unstable and crazy. I had become angry, tired, sad, and defeated. Insecurity was making me say things I would never say, make choices I would never make, and spend money I didn't have. All because I was believing a lie about my own worth.

One morning I was trying to speed things along while we were getting ready, and I told Lexie Beth to jump in my shower. I got the water temperature ready for her and asked her to get in. "Hang on a minute, Mom. I have to weigh myself." That seemed absolutely absurd coming out of her little mouth, and then I realized she had seen me doing the same thing every day for a year. Strip down, step on the scale, and determine my worth. I've always heard it said that what we do in moderation, our kids will do in excess, but watching it play out broke my heart. If I kept going down this path, my daughter would bear the scars of a mom who was living in anything but the freedom Christ came to give.

Insecurity left unchecked grows, like the mold on leftovers at the back of the fridge. It may be out of sight and out of mind, but it will be dealt with at some point and the consequences will be much more significant then. Not only will it grow, but it is horribly contagious. Our children are walking around like little sponges, constantly soaking in and trying to decide what is truly important about them. They're asking, *Where do my parents, my teachers, my friends, and my world tell me identity comes from, and how am I stacking up?* Helping our children develop a healthy foundation for their worth is a tremendous responsibility. Make no mistake, this isn't an area of neutrality in the spiritual realm, and powerful currents are sweeping through our nations.

Who Do You Think You Are?

The Enemy's tactics can be a little squirrely and hard to pin down and identify, especially when we are in the middle of living our story. However, his attempts to make the children of God question their identity as children of God are anything but subtle. If Satan tried to slide a wedge between Jesus and His Father by asking Jesus to prove to be God's legitimate Son, we should expect the same tactic in the lives of our children.

Jesus had just been baptized by John the Baptist. It had been a struggle to get John to agree at first, because John knew full well that Jesus was the Lamb of God, who had come to take away the sins of the world (John 1:29). Who in their right mind feels qualified to baptize the Messiah? Jesus came up out of the water and saw the Holy Spirit descend like a dove. The Father said, "This is my beloved Son, with whom I am well pleased" (Matthew 3:17). If there would have ever been a doubt in Jesus's perfect mind about His identity, if His mother's story about the angel's visit and the virgin conception would have ever made Him wonder, this would have been the moment when all that were laid to rest. God declared over Jesus, "You are my very, very loved Son and I'm so pleased with You."

However, immediately following, the Holy Spirit led Jesus into the wilderness to be tempted by the devil. That's what the Bible text says. I always thought that seemed wrong, as though temptation was a Satan-planned thing. But God was orchestrating this little showdown. "After fasting forty days and forty nights, he was hungry" (Matthew 4:2). You think? Jesus's body depleted, His memory of the baptism beginning to fade, Satan approaches Him with one real question: "Who do you think you are?"

The tempter came and said to him, "If you are the Son of God, command these stones to become loaves of bread" (Matthew 4:3).

"*If* you *are* the Son of God." Prove it. Friends, Satan knew exactly who Jesus was. The question was, did Jesus know deeply who He was and what His mission was? The first temptation Jesus faced during His wilderness experience was echoed in the last He faced—the temptation to prove His deity. When mockers stood at the foot of the cross, hurling insults, they said,

> "*If* you are the Son of God, come down from the cross." So also the chief priests, with the scribes and elders, mocked him, saying, "He saved others; he cannot save himself. He is the King of Israel; let him come down now from the cross, and we will believe in him. He trusts in God; let God deliver him now, if he desires him. For he said, 'I am the Son of God'" (Matthew 27:40-43).

Prove it, they said.

Don't we know that if Jesus's life and ministry were bookended by the temptation to doubt His Sonship that our children will inevitably be tempted to doubt theirs as well? The temptation is far less obvious but poisonous nonetheless. From self-condemnation that says, "If I were a child of God, I wouldn't struggle with this temptation" to the bullying they will encounter that could lead them to believe they are less than wonderfully made, the attacks will be powerful. We cannot protect them from every fiery arrow; we must train them to lift their own shields of faith and believe God on their own. They must believe to their cores that their identity is in Christ, and that like Christ, they rest secure in that unshakable identity.

> Satan is aiming right at the heart of the identity of our children.
>
> —Dr. Nicole McDonald

One powerful force at work in America today is the idea that people, especially children, have the right to self-define. This is so scary for a couple of reasons. First, if we believe we have the right to define ourselves, then we set the standards for our lives. Second, if we define ourselves, then every little thing can be redefined, including our gender. When my parents told me I could be anything I wanted to be, they meant I could choose my career path. Be what you want to be has an entirely different meaning to this generation.

This year the Board of Education in our state recommended that, beginning in kindergarten, children should be given the freedom to choose the gender they want to identify with while at school, without the consent or knowledge of their parents. I have often joked with my husband that some days our youngest son thinks he's a dump truck and has an imaginary friend. What does that say about his competence in deciding his sexuality? And why are we discussing the sexuality of elementary school students anyway?

While I find the whole idea of bypassing parents appalling, we can't miss that the area under intense pressure right now is down to the very heart of how God made us. He created us male and female. The Enemy is frantic to mar the creation of God and to question His goodness toward His children. The same tactic used in the garden of Eden—"Did God actually say...?" (Genesis 3:1)—is unveiled to our children: "Did God actually say you are a boy? Did God make a mistake when He created you? What about *your* feelings? God is holding out on you."

The big lie is that our children will have freedom when they have choices. However, God says if we give Him our choices and trust Him, we will find freedom. Let me promise that no matter how much pain exists in the confusion over gender identity, that the pathway through to health and peace will not come by reassigning our gender. The healing will come as we yield to Christ and trust Him.

If we don't want to define ourselves, then we live in a world that will be happy to define us to meet their ends. If our eyes are open, we will see the infinite organizations, brands, messages, and forces trying to influence the identities of our families. Robert McGee, in his book *The Search for Significance*, says Satan is constantly about the business of "deceiving people, including many Christians, into believing that the basis of their worth is their performance and their ability to please others."[1] McGee believes the Enemy's powerful deception is based on the following formula:

Self Worth = Performance + Others' Opinions[2]

What do we see in society that feeds this satanic formula? This generation will be the Facebook generation, the first group to have their words immediately evaluated by their peers in a public and permanent format. Magazines sell Photoshop-modified and computer-enhanced beauty because any flaw is unacceptable. On the bottom of every receipt is now a phone number we can call to answer questions about our experience and the job performance of the person in front of us, which could make every encounter service providers have nerve-racking. Even when walking through airport security you can often tap a button rating your experience in the inspection process. We understand the desire for constant improvement and satisfaction, but an unhealthy by-product is an incessant process of critically evaluating our performances based on the opinions of others. Just as destructive is the drive to evaluate others that all this builds inside of us.

The problem is this is leading to adults and children who are constantly comparing themselves to others. However, 2 Corinthians 10:12 tells us "When they measure themselves by themselves and compare themselves with themselves, they are not wise" (NIV). Comparison quickly leads to envy, discontentment, striving, anger, and resentment. I have seen my fair share of high school juniors and seniors who are trying to find their worth in GPAs, college acceptance letters, and scholarships. If any of us rely on our performance as the basis of our worth, we will inevitably be led to stress and anxiety as we try to keep the performance going—and to depression because we will ultimately fail. We can even identify the hurt and burnout in our children. And even inside the church, as this way of thinking grows, we become less confident as we serve the Lord, our priorities skew, and we end up relying on our own strength.

Folks, none of these things sounds like the abundant life Christ has promised to His children.

Before we move on to how we should build our children's identity, I need to point out one other area parents need to reflect on. Don't worry, I'm feeling convicted too. Many of us are wrapping up our own identities in our children and calling it love. It's easy to see this play out in parents who push their children in academics and sports to the point of breaking. I've heard other parents whisper at sports games, "They're living the life they always wanted through their daughter." We may even know that pride in ourselves is wrong, but we can mask our puffing up as we bask in the glory of our children.

I know this temptation. I fight it all the time. It's easy for me to feel like a success or a failure as a mother based on the performance and attitudes of my children. Recently, I was teaching on this very topic and said to the women in the audience, "Turn to your neighbor and say, 'Your identity is not dependent on your children.'" They all followed my directive, and afterward two women came up to me, weeping. The first was a woman whose husband served in leadership in their church and whose son was serving time in jail for his poor choices. She told me she needed to be told she wasn't a failure. She isn't a failure because of the poor choices her son made any more than she would be a success if her son had made stellar choices.

The second woman hugged me and whispered that her son was living in a homosexual relationship and that she felt so lost. I held her and we cried together, and I reminded her that her identity was unshakable. Our worth does not come from our children. Our success cannot be tied to the choices our kids make. Our heart strings aren't long enough for that.

Is There Another Way?

Yes, a thousand times yes, there is another way for all of us. But it requires laying aside that old satanic formula of finding self-worth in performance and others' opinions and truly embracing the reality of our triple worth. The truth of God's Word allows you to say, "I have worth because God made me and chose to set His affection on me. This decision was made before I had done anything of worth. I have double worth because not only was I created dearly loved, but I was redeemed by Christ. God proved the depth of His love for me and my children when He sacrificed His Son to redeem us. John 3:16 says, 'For God so loved the world, that he gave his only Son, that whoever believes in him should not perish but have eternal life.' And as if that wasn't enough, I have even greater worth because, after accepting Christ as my Savior, I was given the Holy Spirit. A part of God Himself dwells inside me, offering infinite value."

Many, many of us know this truth in our heads, but the reality of our worth as a child of God should leave us speechless and amazed. Living in the full knowledge of this triple worth is what must build the foundation of our children's identities—not what they do, but that they were fearfully and wonderfully made, and then redeemed and given the Spirit.

As parents, we must whisper over our kids, "You are so well made by God. He loves you so much. Nothing you do can make Him love you less. He loved you so much He gave Jesus for you. You have an indescribable treasure inside you." That's what they need to be raised hearing. In whatever ways our actions or our words have tied them to another source of identity and worth, we need to ask for forgiveness and release them.

Healthy Self-Worth Formula

I knew there had to be a healthy self-worth formula, but for a while I was at a loss even as I looked at Scripture. This declaration from an old *Saturday Night Live* skit couldn't be a workable, daily affirmation: "I'm good enough, I'm smart enough, and doggone it, people like me." I'm not good enough and neither are my kids. And not only are we not smart enough, but there may be a day when no one likes us. Further, we don't want to be puffed up vessels, nor people who falsely believe that to have a right view of self means we can't lift our heads.

Now I know a healthy self-worth formula looks like this:

> Knowing who God says I am +
> Believing what He says is true +
> Acting on what I believe = Healthy Self-Worth

For my children to know who God says they are, I need to teach them who God says they are. This includes being a child of God (John 1:12), Christ's friend (John 15:15), a saint (Ephesians 1:1), free from condemnation (Romans 8:1-2), God's coworker (2 Corinthians 6:1), dearly loved by Him (John 3:16, Isaiah 43:4), and so many, many more precious promises. These are all found in the truth of God's Word, but what we both know is that although this may be truth we know in our heads, it may not have sunk deep into our hearts. And that's where believing comes in. Belief is when we tell our feelings that what they feel is not necessarily a reflection of capital *T* Truth. Belief finds its footing when we choose to act on what we believe is true.

Friends, the Enemy has a strategy: weak moms growing weak kids. The terrific news is that God has a strategy as well and it is infinitely more powerful: free moms raising free kids. This is tied up in our knowing the truth, however. "You will know the truth, and the truth will set you free" (John 8:32).

Powerhouses

What could happen if our children walk into their schools, new environments, and futures believing God has done His best work on them? What if they deeply absorb Ephesians 2:10? "We are God's masterpiece. He has created us anew in Christ Jesus, so we can do the good things he planned for us long ago" (Ephesians 2:10 NLT).

Our children will truly be an unstoppable force for good in the kingdom of God if they believe they have triple worth in the Lord. If they believe they have been gifted by Christ for His glory, and that their worth is not attached to performance or others' opinions, they can be powerhouses in the kingdom of God. Rather than hiding, shrinking back, or trying to self-define, they will be salt in a generation that needs preservation and the flavor of Christ, and a city on a hill in the dark, hurting world.

Let's say to them, you aren't worth more if you're on the honor roll, make the football team, or have lots of friends. You aren't worth less if you have average grades, don't make a sports team, and have only a few friends. You aren't worth more if you win a scholarship. You aren't worth less if you don't win any prizes—or don't even attend college.

And we can model this concept by believing the same about ourselves. We aren't worth more or less because of our performance or other people's opinion either. We simply have worth. Triple worth. And people who believe that can become world changers who take God at His word and freely invest in the lives of others.

> *Good Father,*
> *Thank You for the care You took when You created my children. I praise You and thank You for the creativity You showed as You fashioned their bodies, personalities, and giftings. Help me to cultivate the design You have already written on their lives. Please protect them from the Enemy, who actively seeks to mislead them. Help us know, believe, and act on what You have said about us and to see ourselves through Your eyes. In Christ's name I pray, amen.*

18

Cast Vision

*As far back as I can remember, my mother would have me
down by the bed at night with her, praying. I can still hear
her voice calling my name to God and telling him that she
wanted me to follow him in whatever he called me to do.*
—CHARLES R. SWINDOLL

Our friend Ryan was fading. His skin was turning yellow as his liver
failed to keep up, and his handsome, chiseled features were now gaunt
from the weight loss the cancer had induced. A bag of donated blood
dripped into him because Ryan was now bleeding internally. The
doctors had agreed to one more procedure and one more surgery to
try to extend his life. No one wanted to quit fighting. You can't quit
fighting to save the life of a 27-year-old with a wife and a two-year-
old son—you just can't.

Mike and I had held each other the night before in a hotel room
next to the hospital. We had traveled hours to be beside our friends
as they took the last few steps of Ryan's life. As we entered the room,
his low drawl met us.

"Hey, guys."

"Hey, bud."

We slid into the chairs pulled up at the foot of his bed and talked
Tigers baseball and about how hungry he was from the mandated fast

before surgery. Ryan had a charm about him that was so useful in the kingdom of God and that quickly transitioned strangers into friends. When the doctor walked in to discuss the surgery, Mike and I began to scoot our chairs back to make a quick exit. That's when Ryan said words I will remember the rest of my life. "No, you guys stay. I want you here. You're a part of my inner circle." Oh, the honor of being a part of a hero's inner circle. Though Ryan was years younger than we were, we cherished this stubborn, faith-filled, spent-for-Jesus kid. The next three days were precious agony. They were long and hard and they etched into our minds. Because Ryan was so weak and his body so depleted, the doctors told us he may never wake up from the initial procedure, let alone survive surgery. We watched Ryan say goodbye to Kendra and their son, Colton, twice. The morning of that first procedure, Kendra pulled Colton onto his daddy's lap and Ryan put on the bravest face I've seen. He kissed his son and then commissioned that boy in a way none of us will ever forget. "Colton, you are a cowboy."

Truth be told, Ryan was the cowboy. He left home one summer in high school to work on a Wyoming ranch and came back to Michigan a cowboy. Kendra tells me he left dressed like a jock and came home with a completely new identity, complete with new apparel. Dressing like a cowboy, acting like a cowboy, and spending time developing leadership skills was a different modus operandi than most high schoolers and youth group kids they knew adopted. Ryan seemed to have lost the desire to please people and instead became completely committed to the direction in which he felt led by the Lord. By the time we met Ryan and Kendra, they were in full-time camping ministry and he was one of the most ministry-minded individuals we had ever met. Oh, how we loved nights laughing and talking together. Our sons were born a month apart and that solidified our forever friendship.

When Kendra sat Colton on his father's lap that day, Colton had on his black cowboy boots and his big 'ole belt buckle was fastened on his jeans. He was the spitting image of his dad. "Colton, you are a cowboy." He spent the next few minutes holding his boy and commissioning that two-year-old to be a man of honor. Colton would become a Christ follower who lived close to the Lord, he would defend the defenseless and work hard. Ryan whispered pride over his son, and his gratitude for being his dad. He communicated a knowing that the Lord would be faithful to Colton even though his earthly father might not be with him. Then with tears rolling down his cheeks and that deep voice cracking, he said good-bye and Mike and I took Colton out of the room.

It was brutal, but it was right. Heaven knows that's what brave parents do—the hard thing—the commissioning and the releasing of their children with great expectation—to fulfill the destiny God has in store.

The Power of Blessing

"I believe in you and I believe in the ministry God has ahead of you. You will be a powerful voice in the next generation for the glory of God. You are filled with the Spirit. You are called. You are brave. You have been equipped for the road ahead."

Those are powerful words and they were spoken over me. The result of those words over my life is part of the reason you hold this book in your hands. Sometimes the Lord uses people to look right into your soul and call out the hero and purpose inside you.

> Our children need us to believe God created them to know Him, walk faithfully, and serve Him boldly in the next generation.

Jesus certainly did that when He began calling His disciple Simon Peter another name, Petros—or rock—before he was anything but stable. God called Gideon a mighty warrior while he threshed wheat in a winepress, hiding from the enemy. Likewise, our children need us to believe God created them to know Him, walk faithfully, and serve

Him boldly in the next generation. He is in the process of using us to equip them with everything they need to accomplish His purposes in the next generation and He plans on keeping them through it all.

Blessing is "the intentional act of speaking God's favor and power into someone's life, often accompanied by a symbolic gesture such as laying hands on the person."[1] When Paul's death drew near, he wrote one final note to his dear Timothy. The letter was meant to fill Timothy with a reminder of Paul's love, but also to remind him that he had a powerful role to play in the next generation.

> I remind you to fan into flame the gift of God, which is in you through the laying on of my hands, for God gave us a spirit not of fear but of power and love and self-control. Therefore do not be ashamed of the testimony about our Lord, nor of me his prisoner, but share in suffering for the gospel by the power of God, who saved us and called us to a holy calling, not because of our works but because of his own purpose and grace (2 Timothy 1:6-9).

> What you heard from me, keep as the pattern of sound teaching, with faith and love in Christ Jesus. Guard the good deposit that was entrusted to you—guard it with the help of the Holy Spirit who lives in us (2 Timothy 1:13-14 NIV).

Paul tells Timothy, "The things I have shown you, the pattern of my life—live that way." Oh that we would be able to say the same. Let's commission our children for the next generation and believe with unwavering hope that God will use them. Because He will. He will use our messy BRAVE to model it first and then equip them to move forward as heroes of the faith in the next generation. Our belief will be the catapult that launches them there, and our prayers to the Father will cling to them as they go.

The Race

It all felt right. We slid out of bed and grabbed our running clothes. I tied my hair back in a messy bun and decided makeup was overrated. As we began to slip down the stairs—quietly to avoid waking the two who would stay behind—two of the hall doors opened, revealing Brendan and Lexie Beth. We all smiled at each other. Soon, in hushed tones, Brendan was talking to his dad about strategy for the race ahead.

It was a quick drive to the starting point of the race, and as we pulled in we began to see familiar faces. Friends we love were climbing out of their cars with their kids, and the reminder of the depth of relationship we have in this little rural spot filled me to the brim with love. We registered and went to look at the map of the course hanging nearby. We would warm up as a family, and so we slowly began to loosen our muscles and prepare our minds.

Each of us had a race plan. Mine was simply to run to the finish filled with joy. Mike's goal involved survival, keeping his bad knees in check and somehow keeping up with our middle schooler. Lexie Beth also had a plan. She would run to the finish as fast as she could. I kept reminding her this race included grown-ups who may not slow down for her and that she hadn't been running regularly for a couple of months.

"Just do your best," I said. "I love you guys." And then they were off.

My family pulled ahead and I watched them begin at a speed I knew I could never maintain. My race has always been different, more reflective, more for the joy of running and the camaraderie on the course than for speed. I watched my breathing and centered my thoughts on the beauty of the morning and the worship music in my earbuds.

After the initial quarter mile, the mob of people began to thin, and as I rounded the corner I caught a glimpse of Mike and Brendan. Much of the trail was difficult terrain. About halfway through the race I ran into a clearing where I could watch participants run down into a valley and then up a wall of a hill. It was straight up and every one of us would be forced to dig deep. That's when I saw Lexie Beth up ahead. The course would make a switchback and I would have the chance to watch her run from a distance far behind.

Lexie is a runner. When she was four, we went to a Relay for Life Walk-a-Thon at a local high school to watch Ryan speak about the cancer experience from the perspective of someone in the middle of the journey. The kids were all given necklaces to wear, and for every lap they made around the track, they received a bead for their necklace. Little Lexie ran three miles in a pair of flip-flops before we realized she was enjoying herself and not simply gathering beads. Little has changed; she runs for the joy of the race, the thrill of competition, and the glory of the finish.

As I began the descent into the valley, I could see Mike and Brendan still running strong side by side, and ahead of them the little frame of my nine-year-old runner. Her ponytail swished and her strides were strong. As we switched back I knew she was finally close enough to hear me. I cheered, "Good job, baby girl! Go, go, go!" Her face was hot and sweaty and determined. Ahead of her was the hill we would all face, and I knew my goal of just keeping my own pace at a jog was going to be difficult. Lexie hit the bottom of the hill and leaned in, digging deep to charge forward. She looked so small and the hill seemed so large and unfair, but as she crested the hill, my spirit soared. Several minutes later I would face the same hill, fighting with every step, the memory of watching my daughter running propelling me slowly up.

We finished the course in three separate waves. Lexie alone and in the front, Brendan and Mike side by side (the knee held out), and me several minutes behind. As I crossed the finish line, my tribe had already circled back to congratulate me and cheer me on. All four of us were filled with joy and pride for each other.

Friends, this *is* our time on the course. It's dark, the path is uneven, and at times it may not even seem fair. And yet we run. For a brief while we will have our children tucked in at our side, learning, stumbling, and keeping pace with us. If we are blessed, we will have time when we can keep up with them and run alongside, despite our aching knees. But at some point in the future we will let go and hope for a glimpse at a switchback.

> Since we are surrounded by such a great cloud of witnesses, let us throw off everything that hinders and the sin that so easily entangles. And let us run with perseverance the race marked out for us (Hebrews 12:1 NIV).

BRAVE mama, I'm honored to have run this lap with you. Fix your eyes on Jesus and run on. The prize will be glorious.

Father,
My family belongs to You. We were created for Your glory, to bring You praise. I recommit myself to raising children who fulfill that purpose. I pray that my home will be full of Your praises, Your Word, and Your Spirit. Renew my passion and energy to raise children who are faithful to Your call in public and in private. Cultivate in me faithfulness as I seek to discern the best use of the time I have with them in my care. Make these lessons be true in me and then in them. Use my children for the purposes You have for them and help me to be brave as You call them to step out. I commit them to You and entrust them into Your hands, believing with all my heart that You are worth it. In Jesus's name, amen.

A Word to the Grandmas

Dear Grandma,

They may call you Meema or Gi-Gi or Nani or Granny or G-maw, but regardless of your title the role you've been given by the Lord is precious and important. If you have read to this point in the book, I want you to know I see your commitment to the next generation, and it inspires me.

May I make three brief suggestions to you as a grandmom from the perspective of a mom in the trenches?

1. Let Faith Dwell First in You

The influence of one grandmother in Scripture helped change the course of history, and thank the Lord we have her name. Sometimes that doesn't happen, either in Scripture or in life in general, I suppose. Lois was a woman of deep faith in Yahweh. As a Jewess, she was waiting for the Messiah to come and she found strength in the Scriptures. Her daughter, Eunice, was also a woman of faith, but had married a Greek man. I imagine Lois wasn't comfortable with their marriage if she was a devout Jew, but we can know for sure that no matter her hang-ups about her son-in-law, she fell in love with the grandchild that union brought her. At some point, maybe during Paul's trip to Lystra, her hometown, or maybe from new believers coming home from Jerusalem, Lois and Eunice learned about Christ.

Lois embraced the teachings of Christ with her daughter and began teaching her grandson the Jewish Scriptures and how they were fulfilled in Jesus. Paul wrote to the young man,

> Continue in what you have learned and have firmly
> believed, knowing from whom you learned it and how
> *from childhood* you have been acquainted with the sacred
> writings, which are able to make you wise for salvation
> through faith in Christ Jesus (2 Timothy 3:14-15, empha-
> sis added).

That young man was Timothy, Paul's dearest companion and son in the faith. We really can't emphasize how incredible the contribution of those two women were to the ministry of Paul. They had nurtured and faithfully discipled the young Timothy, so that when God presented the opportunity for ministry, he was ready in body and spirit. That boy went on to become a mighty warrior in the kingdom of God, and as Paul reminded him in his final letter,

> I am reminded of your sincere faith, a faith that dwelt
> first in your grandmother Lois and your mother Eunice
> and now, I am sure, dwells in you as well (2 Timothy 1:5).

Let's link arms and train our children in the Scriptures from hearts that are well watered in the Word.

2. Try to Stay Involved

As we said before, there is power in presence.

Your relationship with your grandchildren may be close. While my in-laws were preparing to head to the mission field, they stayed in the home of one of their parents. Before their departure for Indonesia and upon their return home, Mike's grandparents played a tremendously important role in his life. Your story may be difficult, like theirs, and you may be standing in the gap for your kids in the lives of your grandchildren. That is certainly the case in many homes. If so, receive my admiration and prayers. You may attend soccer games in the rain, listen to squeaky instruments at band concerts, or even let them drive your car to prom. All of it matters.

This role may change as the years roll on. I had the opportunity to live with Mike's grandparents for several months when we were engaged. It was a unique privilege to live in such a mature, nurturing, godly environment. Some of my sweetest memories are coming in from a date with their grandson and climbing onto the foot of their bed to talk. Grandpa still likes to tease me that they couldn't keep me out, but I know they loved it too. What a gift I received watching them love each other, study Scripture, and live their lives to honor Christ. It was an unconventional role—adopted grandparents—but it all mattered.

Or, sadly, you may not be present in the lives of your children and grandchildren at all. Perhaps your relationship with your children hit the rocks, or you were distracted for a time. Whatever the reason for the space and tension, you can lead the way in trying to rebuild a bridge. Relationships take effort, and they are messy and hard. But this grandparenting stuff is worth it, for you and for them.

My parents live 14 hours' and 21 hours' drive away from Michigan. It would be easy for them to believe that the space between us absolves them of the responsibility they have in building relationships with my kids. I'm grateful for the time and energy they spend developing those special bonds with them. Their care packages, notes of encouragement, telling us silly things that remind them of our kids, and making phone calls make the difference when the miles are great.

Impressions can be made by hard blows or frequent exposure. The world is dealing us all enough hard blows right now. Let's opt for frequent, loving, faith-filled exposure in the lives of those we love. It all matters.

3. Pray as If It All Depends on You

If we have come this far together and I still haven't convinced you that your prayers matter so much, I don't know what else I can say. The greatest gift you could give your children and grandchildren is your prayers. Consistent, earnest prayers for their faith in this generation will make a difference, because our God hears and answers. Spend the time to make a systematic and scriptural list of the areas of life your grandchildren face. Pray those deep and brave hero prayers, and ask for faith-filled followers of Christ in your lineage of faith until Christ's return.

> I tell you, whatever you ask in prayer, believe that you have received it, and it will be yours (Mark 11:24).

May your grandchildren walk in the way of Christ, devoted to Him and prepared by Him. No amount of time spent loving your grandchildren and pointing them to Jesus is wasted, and that's a promise. Your kids may never say it, but we are grateful for your standing in the gap. Thank you for loving our kids enough to read a book about raising them to know Jesus. May He be honored and glorified in us, and may all *your generations* be represented before the throne of Him who loves us.

With great faith,

Lee

Hope for the Mothers of Prodigals

Dear Friend,

Last night we had a terrible evening with our son and I thought of you. It occurred to me that at one time in your life, you held your child and felt the bliss of motherhood. You probably inhaled the sweet smell of babyhood mixed with Baby Magic lotion, or sunblock on the smell of a sweaty, growing child, and reveled in the delight of being a mama. My guess is that in those sweet days you never imagined you would end up at this heartbroken place.

Recently, I was driving down the highway when I spotted a huge something on the shoulder of my side of the road. It was roughly the size of an end table in my living room, obviously an unmistakable obstacle. As my car approached it, the image began to clear. It was a large, beautiful bald eagle eating roadkill. It took about 30 seconds to register what I had just seen, and a few more to turn my head to my friend and ask, "Was that a bald eagle?"

"Yes. I think so."

It was so appalling and disturbing that I turned my head and said, "Don't you know who you are? Roadkill is so beneath you." It was such a waste of breathtaking beauty, power, and majesty. Eagles are meant to soar and snatch fish while in flight, not pick at bloated remains.

I imagine this is how you feel as a parent, so disappointed as you watch your child make choices beneath his or her position as a child of the Most High God. BRAVE moms call out the best and the brave in their children, but sometimes it doesn't happen right away and sometimes our very best doesn't lead where we hoped, dreamed, or imagined. If we were together, I'd wrap you up in a hug and we'd cry and agree your child was made for so much more.

I have a few things I hope you'll think and pray over.

First, I'm so sorry. Your child walking away from the Lord, and maybe even you, was not what you planned. It hurts. It has cost you tears, heartache, relationships, dignity, and may have even affected your marriage. Children walking away from the Lord is the stuff of broken dreams, and no matter their age, rebellious and wayward kids grieve us. You can be confident, however, that you don't grieve alone. Our heavenly Father has called Himself our comforter, counselor, and healer. Run to Him and draw your strength and hope from the source who will never fail.

Second, I want to point you back to reflection and prayer. This time the question I hold before you is one of eternal consequence but which may hurt to answer. Has your child *ever* given proof of his or her salvation? If so, let's pray fervently that the Holy Spirit will have His way in your child. If not, we must circle back around and beg the Lord to open your child's eyes and turn them from darkness to light.

I heard an interview with Ruth Bell Graham, the wife of evangelist Billy Graham. She was discussing raising their five children. Two of those children were prodigals. She described praying for her sons' return to the Lord, but also about needing wisdom to separate moral issues from non-moral issues. She described moral issues like lying, stealing, cheating, and disrespect, versus non-moral issues like tracking dirt into the house.[1] In essence, she was encouraging moms to choose their battles wisely, and I would suggest that sometimes we major on habits and outward manifestations rather than praying deeply into the core moral issues that need to be addressed in the lives of our children. Let's spend the time with the Lord necessary to quiet our hearts and gain His perspective.

Last, scan the horizon expectantly. Our hearts try to guard themselves from hurt by forming a callus over our wounded hearts.

However, callused hearts stop us from enjoying the good as well, and do not produce the life of joy and hope that can come from the Holy Spirit. You probably know the story from Luke 15, the parable of the prodigal son and the father who loved him. Don't underestimate God's ability to relate to your heart, friend. As Ruth Graham said, "God has trouble with His children too," and He does.[5] Our Father knows the pain you experience as you watch your child pull away, and He knows what it's like to see His children live neck-deep in sin and slop.

God hears your prayers and feels the pain. We can rest assured that He is hunting down your children, relentlessly. Because, like the shepherd in the parable of the lost sheep, He will search to rescue even one, and because, like the woman in the parable of the lost coin, He will turn everything upside down looking for the lost (Luke 15:1-10), we know He's listening to our prayers and working in our children's lives. Follow the example of the father in the parable of the prodigal son and watch expectantly for your child's return. Point your chair to the north and scan the horizon. "While he was still a long way off, his father saw him and felt compassion, and ran and embraced and kissed him" (Luke 15:20).

Friend, God is still working miracles. I just stood behind the wall of a baptismal and watched a prodigal make a public declaration of her faith. The road has been marked with suffering, and some long-lasting consequences are likely, but God is making all things new.

Plan the welcome home party and wait expectantly.

Believing with you,

Lee

Reflection Questions

General (Personality)
- What are my child's greatest strengths?
- Do I perceive any persistent weaknesses?
- What do they enjoy right now?
- What is their behavior style (introvert or extrovert, task driven or social)?
- How do they recharge, and are they getting enough time to do so?
- What is their love language, and how do they show love?
- When do they feel successful or defeated?

Character
- What is their hot button?
- Can I trust them to be honest?
- Is obedience to authority a priority to them?
- Is my child learning to be diligent in his or her tasks and work with a cheerful heart?
- Are they quick to repent and ask forgiveness?
- Is my child learning to practice self-control (anger, food, exercise, emotions, sexuality)?

Faith
- Do I know they are saved?
- Do I see fruit of that decision?
- What is their spiritual pathway (how do they connect with the Lord)?
- Can I discern my child's spiritual gifts and how have I seen him or her used by the Lord?
- Is my child spending time in the Word of God?

Vision
- What do I think they may be in the future?
- What talents do they have?
- Am I regularly expressing excitement to my child about the future the Lord has for him or her?

Education/Self-Care
- What is my child's learning style?
- What are their academic strengths and weaknesses?
- Do I know of any regular fears or things that cause my child anxiety?
- Is my child learning and practicing age-appropriate hygiene?
- Do I have health concerns for them?

Relationships
- Who does my child connect with in this season (parents, teachers, coaches, pastors)?
- Describe the relationship with each parent in this season.
- Who are my child's closest friends, and what kind of influence are they having on my child?
- What kind of influence is my child on others?
- What do I know about their relationship with opposite sex and what do they need to learn?

Action
- As I review these answers to these questions, what do I need to cultivate in my child right now?
- As I consider this season, do I sense any promptings from the Lord related to this child?
- Is there something I need to teach them right now (about God, about life, about themselves, about others)?
- Is there a new habit I need to help them develop or encourage them to break?
- Is there an attitude that needs to be challenged or encouraged?
- What do I need to commit to prayer?
- What are three words I would like to be used to describe this child?

Notes

Chapter 1: Where Are All the Heroes?

1. "Definition of Dissonance in English," http://www.oxforddictionaries
.com/us/definition/american_english/dissonance.

2. "Christopher Reeve Quotes," http://www.brainyquote.com/quotes/
authors/c/christopher_reeve.html.

Chapter 2: The Mama Prayer and When FEAR Sets In

1. Jack Canfield, Mark Victor Hansen, and Amy Newmark, *Chicken Soup
for the Soul: Home Sweet Home: 101 Stories about Hearth, Happiness, and
Hard Work* (Cos Cob, CT: Chicken Soup for the Soul, 2014), 351.

Chapter 3: Fear Left Unchecked

1. E. E. Carpenter, and P. W. Comfort, *Holman Treasury of Key Bible
Words: 200 Greek and 200 Hebrew Words Defined and Explained* (Nashville, TN: Broadman & Holman Publishers, 2000), 60.

2. CalmClinic, "Anxiety and the Brain: An Introduction," accessed
November 1, 2016, http://www.calmclinic.com/anxiety/anxiety-brain.

Chapter 4: The Fumbled Torch

1. Erin's actual name was changed to respect her identity. Erin means
"peace" in Gaelic.

2. Bundolo, "Olympic 2010 Torch Drop in North Vancouver," https://
www.youtube.com/watch?v=YyIzLKcdprw.

Chapter 5: The Beautiful Surrender

1. Kelly Minter, *No Other Gods: Confronting Our Modern Day Idols* (Colorado Springs, CO: David C Cook, 2008), 14.

2. John Piper, *Adoniram Judson: How Few There Are Who Die So Hard!*
(Minneapolis, MN: Desiring God Foundation, 2012), 12.

Chapter 6: Believe God

1. Edward W. Goodrick, and John R. Kohlenberger III, *Zondervan NIV Exhaustive Concordance, 2*nd *Edition* (Grand Rapids, MI: Zondervan, 1999), 2577.

2. Revelation 19:15.

3. Beth Moore, *Believing God: Experiencing a Fresh EXPLOSION of Faith* (Nashville, TN: LifeWay Press, 2004), 7.

4. *Raising Children Who Hope in the Triumph of God*, "Will the Next Generation Know?" written by John Piper, *Desiring God*, July 25, 1982.

5. William Hendriksen, *New Testament Commentary: Mark* (Grand Rapids, MI: Baker Book House, 1975).

Chapter 7: Reflect

1. *Holy Bible English Standard Version, Brown, Trutone* (Wheaton, IL: Crossway Books, 2008), 336.

Chapter 8: Ask Forgiveness

1. *The Most Important Place on Earth*, The Most Important Place on Earth, Day 2, by Robert Wolgemuth, *Revive Our Hearts Radio*, July 26, 2016.

2. Albert Barnes, "Commentary on Psalms 139:4," Barnes' Notes on the New Testament, www.studylight.org/commentaries/bnb/psalms-139 .html. 1870.

3. Dorothy Briggs, *Your Child's Self-Esteem* (New York, NY: Doubleday, 1975), 65.

4. Charles W. Colson, *Born Again: What Really Happened to the White House Hatchet Man* (Grand Rapids, MI: Baker Book House, 1976), 14.

5. Emily Colson, *Dancing with Max: A Mother and Son Who Broke Free* (Grand Rapids, MI: Zondervan, 2010), 17.

6. Colson, *Born Again*, 337.

7. Chris Colson, "My Father's Incarceration Was a Gift to Millions," *Christian Post Opinion* (2015), accessed October 28, 2016, http://www .christianpost.com/news/chuck-colson-prison-gift-to-millions-152568/.

Chapter 10: Equip Them

1. Sally Michael, *Mothers: Disciplers of the Next Generations* (Minneapolis, MN: Good News Publishers, 2013), 20.

2. Billy Graham Evangelistic Association, 2011, "Ruth Bell Graham—A

Mother's Wisdom," accessed November 1,2016. https://www.youtube
.com/watch?v=y LaIOWEowyY.

Chapter 11: Teach Them to Know and Obey Their God

1. Joseph A. Siess, *Voices from Babylon; or, the Records of Daniel the Prophet* (Philadelphia: The Castle Press), 19.

2. Ibid.

Chapter 12: Teach Them About the Value of the Word of God

1. P. M. Bechtel, and P. W. Comfort, *Who's Who in Christian History* (Wheaton, IL: Tyndale House, 1992), 683–4.

2. Ibid.

3. M. Galli, and T. Olsen, *131 Christians Everyone Should Know* (Nashville, TN: Broadman & Holman Publishers, 2000), 348–50.

Chapter 13: Teach Them to Pray

1. Sonya Shafer, *Laying Down the Rails: A Charlotte Mason Habits Handbook* (Grayson, GA: Simply Charlotte Mason, LLC, 2007), 15.

2. Ann Voskamp, *One Thousand Gifts* (Grand Rapids, MI: Zondervan, 2010), 15.

3. Fern Nichols, *Moms in Prayer: Standing in the Gap for Your Children.* (Grand Rapids, MI: Zondervan, 2013), 100–101.

4. Moms in Prayer International, 2016, "Full Interview with War Room Producer Stephen Kendrick," accessed November 1, 2016. https://www. you tube.com/watch?v=zSHR8nl8ePY.

Chapter 14: Teach Them About Self-Control

1. Charles Spurgeon. *Morning by Morning: A New Edition of the Classic Devotional Based on The Holy Bible, English Standard Version* (Wheaton, IL: Crossway, 2008), 162.

2. "Spotlight: The Sex Lives of Unmarried Evangelicals," *Christianity Today*, May 2013:11.

3. Ibid.

4. John MacArthur, *The MacArthur New Testament Commentary: Romans 1–8* (Chicago, IL: Moody Publishers, 1991), 109.

Chapter 15: Teach Them About Relationships

1. Katie Davis, 2016. *Kisses from Katie*, http://katiedavis.amazima.org.

Chapter 16: Teach Them to Serve

1. Lysa TerKeurst, "The Best Yes" (Conference teaching, She Speaks, Concord, NC, July 25, 2014).

Chapter 17: Teach Them to Find Their Identity in Christ

1. Robert S. McGee, *The Search for Significance: Seeing Your True Worth Through God's Eyes* (Nashville, TN: Thomas Nelson, 1998), 21.

2. Ibid.

Chapter 18: Cast Vision

1. Rolf Garborg, *The Family Blessing* (Dallas: Word Publishing Company, 1990), 13.

Hope for the Mothers of Prodigals

1. Billy Graham Evangelistic Association, 2011, "Ruth Bell Graham—A Mother's Wisdom," accessed November 1, 2016, https://www.youtube.com/watch?v=yLaIOWEowyY.

2. Ibid.

Bibliography

Andrews, Evan. "When Did the White Flag Become Associated with Surrender?" History.com. December 02, 2015. Accessed July 31, 2016. http://www.history.com/news/ask-history/when-did-the-white-flag-become-associated-with-surrender.

Barnes, Albert. "Commentary on Psalms 139:4." "Barnes' Notes on the New Testament." www.studylight.org/commentaries/bnb/psalms-139.html. 1870.

Bechtel, P. M. and P. W. Comfort. *Who's Who in Christian History.* Wheaton, IL: Tyndale House, 1992.

Billy Graham Evangelistic Association, 2011. "Ruth Bell Graham—A Mother's Wisdom." Accessed November 1, 2016. https://www.youtube.com/watch?v=yI_aIOWEowyY.

Branson, Tim. "Frank Peretti: The Man and the 'Monster,'" Christian Broadcasting Network. Accessed October 29, 2016. http://www1.cbn.com/700club/frank-peretti-man-and-monster.

Bundolo. "Olympic 2010 Torch Drop in North Vancouver." YouTube. February 11, 2010. Accessed July 31, 2016. https://www.youtube.com/watch?v=YyIzLKcdprw.

CalmClinic. "Anxiety and the Brain: An Introduction." Accessed November 1, 2016. http://www.calmclinic.com/anxiety/anxiety-brain.

Canfield, Jack, Mark Victor Hansen, and Amy Newmark. *Chicken Soup for the Soul: Home Sweet Home: 101 Stories about Hearth, Happiness, and Hard Work.* Cos Cob, CT: Chicken Soup for the Soul, 2014.

Carpenter, E. E., and Comfort, P. W. *Holman Treasury of Key Bible Words: 200 Greek and 200 Hebrew Words Defined and Explained.* Nashville, TN: Broadman & Holman Publishers, 2000.

"Christopher Reeve Quotes." brainyquote.com. Accessed July 31, 2016.
http://www.brainyquote.com/quotes/authors/c/christopher_reeve.html.

Colson, Charles W. *Born Again: What Really Happened to the White House Hatchet Man.* Grand Rapids: Baker Book House Company, 1976.

Colson, Chris. "My Father's Incarceration Was a Gift to Millions," *Christian Post Opinion (2015).* Accessed October 28, 2016. http://www
.christianpost.com/news/chuck-colson-prison-gift-to-millions-152568/.

Colson, Emily. *Dancing with Max: A Mother and Son Who Broke Free.* Grand Rapids, MI: Zondervan, 2010.

Davis, Katie, 2016. *Kisses from Katie.* http://katiedavis.amazima.org.

"Definition of Dissonance in English." Dissonance: Definition of Dissonance in *Oxford Dictionary* (American English) (US). Accessed July 31, 2016. http://www.oxforddictionaries.com/us/definition/american_english/dissonance.

"Definition of Entrust in English." Entrust: Definition of Entrust in *Oxford Dictionary* (American English) (US). Accessed July 31, 2016. http://www.oxforddictionaries.com/us/definition/american_english/entrust?q=entrusting.

Galli, M. and T. Olsen. *131 Christians Everyone Should Know.* Nashville, TN: Broadman & Holman Publishers, 2000.

Garborg, Rolf. *The Family Blessing.* Dallas: Word Publishing Company, 1990.

Goodrick, Edward W., and John R. Kohlenberger III. *Zondervan NIV Exhaustive Concordance, 2nd Edition.* Grand Rapids, MI: Zondervan, 1999.

Hendriksen, William. *New Testament Commentary: Mark.* Grand Rapids, MI: Baker Book House, 1975.

Holy Bible English Standard Version, Brown, Trutone. Wheaton, IL: Crossway Books, 2008.

MacArthur, John. *The MacArthur New Testament Commentary: Romans 1-8.* Chicago, IL: Moody Publishers, 1991.

McGee, Robert S. *The Search for Significance: Seeing Your TRUE WORTH through God's Eyes.* Nashville, TN: Thomas Nelson, 1998.

Michael, Sally. *Mothers: Disciplers of the Next Generations.* Minneapolis, MN: Good News Publishers, 2013.

Minter, Kelly. *No Other Gods: Confronting Our Modern Day Idols.* Colorado Springs, CO: David C Cook, 2008.

Moms in Prayer International, 2016. "Full Interview with War Room Producer Stephen Kendrick." Accessed on November 1, 2016. https://www.youtube.com/watch?v=zSHR8nl8ePY.

Moore, Beth. *Believing God: Experiencing a Fresh EXPLOSION of Faith.* Nashville, TN: LifeWay Press, 2004.

Nichols, Fern. *Moms in Prayer: Standing in the Gap for Your Children.* Grand Rapids, MI: Zondervan, 2013.

Peretti, Frank. *The Wounded Spirit.* Nashville, TN: Word Publishing, 2000.

Piper, John. *Adoniram Judson: How Few There Are Who Die So Hard!* Minneapolis, MN: Desiring God Foundation, 2012.

Raising Children Who Hope in the Triumph of God. "Will the Next Generation Know?" Written by John Piper. *Desiring God*, July 25, 1982.

Shafer, Sonya. *Laying Down the Rails: A Charlotte Mason Habits Handbook.* Grayson, GA: Simply Charlotte Mason, LLC, 2007.

Siess, Joseph A. *Voices from Babylon; or, the Records of Daniel the Prophet.* Patala Press, 2016.

"Spotlight: The Sex Lives of Unmarried Evangelicals." *Christianity Today.* May 2013:11.

Spurgeon, Charles. *Morning by Morning: A New Edition of the Classic Devotional Based on the Holy Bible, English Standard Version.* Wheaton, IL: Crossway, 2008.

TerKeurst, Lysa. "The Best Yes." Conference teaching, She Speaks, Concord, NC, July 25, 2014.

The Most Important Place on Earth. "The Most Important Place on Earth, Day 2," by Robert Wolgemuth. *Revive Our Hearts Radio*, July 26, 2016.

Voskamp, Ann. *One Thousand Gifts.* Grand Rapids, MI: Zondervan, 2010.

Acknowledgments

Precious Lord—You are the way, the truth and the life, all to You I owe. Every word is for You, and every great thought comes from You. To You be all glory, honor, and praise.

Mike, my farmer—It is a privilege to be your wife and to parent our tribe together. Thank you for loving me and leading me so well. I love, admire, and respect you, and I'm ever so grateful that I am yours. May our walk together bring many to Christ.

Brendan, Gabi, Lexie Beth, and Ryan—There would be no book without you. Thank you for letting me share our story, for forgiving me time and again, and for encouraging me to keep writing. I love you and I'm so grateful to be your mama. Chase after Jesus, I'm cheering you on.

Jeanna—Every step of the way you encouraged me and spurred me on. Chapter 3 wouldn't be in this book if you hadn't told me to chase fear and promised me it would be worth it. Thank you for being my confidant, prayer buddy, and assistant. You are a gift.

Our parents—You give us the roots that have made Mike and me who we are. We laugh harder, love deeper, and love Jesus more because of each of you. I love you.

Our extended family—Being a Ford Tutor Riley Nienhuis is an honor. I love that the Lord gave me each of you.

Marlae and Meltha—My mentors and dear friends. Thank you.

Kathleen Kerr—My editor and friend. You get me and you love Jesus. I'm so glad we chose each other. I hope we strike sparks off each other for a long time.

Harvest House team—Working with you is a delight. Thank you for taking a chance on me.

My pastors and FBC family—You lead me well. Thank you for encouraging and equipping me to teach the Word. I love calling you home and worshipping Jesus with you.

My Grace Adventures family—Thank you for being my friends and my favorite place to serve. For believing Jesus would use me long before I did. I'm keeping my nametag and using it as long as you'll have me.

My Moms in Prayer family—It is an honor to serve beside you. You are the bravest women I know. Every school till Jesus returns.

My hero friends and family who have let me tell their stories— May Jesus be brought even greater glory. Thank you.

Our friends—The ones who ministered through presence, car rides, ice cream cones, confetti, cards, balloons, canned goods, brainstorming, and campfires. To the ones who my kids call big sisters, and the ones who have prayed me through, and who have extended grace upon grace.

About the Author

Lee Nienhuis is a passionate and dynamic Bible teacher and communicator. She serves on the National Speaking Team for Moms in Prayer International and loves serving women at conferences and retreats nationwide. She longs for revival that begins in our hearts, transforms our homes, and impacts our communities. She and her farmer-husband, Mike, have four great kids and live in beautiful West Michigan. Lee *loves* being a wife and mother, but when she isn't carting kids, attending sporting events, or whipping up dinners, she loves hot cups of coffee, deep friendships, and laughing till her sides ache.

You can learn more about Lee, her ministry, and her speaking schedule, and find other resources at

LeeNienhuis.com *or* BraveMomsBraveKids.com

Connect with her online on Facebook, Instagram, and Twitter.